Character Education

Managing Responsibilities

Character Education

Character Education

Managing Responsibilities

MARIE-THERESE MILLER

CONSULTING EDITORS AND INTRODUCTION BY
Madonna M. Murphy, Ph.D.
University of St. Francis

and **Sharon L. Banas**
former Values Education Coordinator,
Sweet Home Central School District, New York

CHELSEA HOUSE
PUBLISHERS
An imprint of Infobase Publishing

Character Education: Managing Responsibilities
Copyright © 2009 by Infobase Publishing

Chelsea House
An imprint of Infobase Publishing
132 West 31st Street
New York NY 10001

Library of Congress Cataloging-in-Publication Data
Miller, Marie-Therese.
  Managing responsibilities / Marie-Therese Miller.
    p. cm. — (Character education)
  Includes bibliographical references and index.
  ISBN 978-1-60413-124-6 (hardcover : alk. paper) 1. Responsibility—
Juvenile literature. 2. Character—Juvenile literature. I. Title.
  BJ1451.M55 2009
  179'.9—dc22   2009001087

Chelsea House books are available at special discounts when purchased in bulk quantities for businesses, associations, institutions, or sales promotions. Please call our Special Sales Department in New York at (212) 967-8800 or (800) 322-8755.

You can find Chelsea House on the World Wide Web at http://www.chelseahouse.com

Text design by Annie O'Donnell
Cover design by Takeshi Takahashi

Printed in the United States

Bang EJB 10 9 8 7 6 5 4 3 2 1

This book is printed on acid-free paper.

All links and Web addresses were checked and verified to be correct at the time of publication. Because of the dynamic nature of the Web, some addresses and links may have changed since publication and may no longer be valid.

CONTENTS

INTRODUCTION

On February 14, 2008, as these books were being edited, a shooting occurred at Northern Illinois University (NIU) in DeKalb, Illinois. A former NIU graduate student, dressed in black and armed with a shotgun and two handguns, opened fire from the stage of a lecture hall. The shooter killed five students and injured 16 others before committing suicide. What could have led someone to do this? Could it have been prevented?

When the shooting started, student Dan Parmenter and his girlfriend, Lauren Debrauwere, who was sitting next to him, dropped to the floor between the rows of seats. Dan covered Lauren with his body, held her hand, and began praying. The shield of Dan's body saved Lauren's life, but Dan was fatally wounded. In that hall, on February 14, 2008—Valentine's Day—one person's deed was horrific and filled with hate; another's was heroic and loving.

The purpose of this series of books is to help prevent the occurrence of this kind of violence by offering readers the character education and social and emotional skills they need to control their emotions and make good moral choices. This series includes books on topics such as coping with bullying, conflicts, peer pressure, prejudice, anger and frustration, and numerous responsibilities, as well as learning how to handle teamwork and respect for others, be fair and honest, and be a good leader and decision-maker.

In his 1992 book, *Why Johnny Can't Tell Right from Wrong,*[1] William Kilpatrick coined the term "moral illiteracy" and dedicated a whole chapter to it. Today, as he points out, people often do not recognize when they are in a situation that calls for a moral choice, and they are not able to define what is right and what is wrong in that situation. The California-based Josephson Institute of Ethics agrees with these concerns. The institute states that we have a "character deficit" in our society today and points out that increasing numbers of young people across the United States—from well-to-do as well as disadvantaged backgrounds—demonstrate reckless disregard for fundamental standards of ethical conduct.

According to the 2006 *Josephson Institute Report Card on the Ethics of American Youth*, our children are at risk. This report sets forth the results of a biannual written survey completed in 2006 by more than 36,000 high school students across the country. The compilers of the report found that 82 percent of the students surveyed admitted that they had lied to a parent about something significant within the previous year. Sixty percent admitted to having cheated during a test at school, and 28 percent admitted to having stolen something from a store.[2] (Various books in this series will tell of other findings in this report.) Clearly, helping young people to develop character is a need of national importance.

The United States Congress agrees. In 1994, in the joint resolution that established National Character Counts Week, Congress declared that "the character of a nation is only as strong as the character of its individual citizens." The resolution also stated that "people do not automatically develop good character and, therefore, conscientious efforts must be made by youth-influencing institutions . . . to help young people develop the essential traits and characteristics that comprise good character."[3]

Many stories can be told of people who have defended our nation with character. One of the editors of this series knew one such young man named Jason Dunham. On April 24, 2004, Corporal Jason L. Dunham was serving with the United States Marines in Iraq. As Corporal Dunham's squad was conducting a reconnaissance mission, the men heard sounds of rocket-propelled grenades and small arms fire. Corporal

Dunham led a team of men toward that fire to assist their battalion commander's ambushed convoy. An insurgent leaped out at Corporal Dunham, and he saw the man release a grenade. Corporal Dunham alerted his team and immediately covered the grenade with his helmet and his body. He lost his own life, but he saved the lives of others on his team.

In January 2007, the Dunham family traveled to Washington, D.C., where President George W. Bush presented them with Corporal Dunham's posthumously awarded Congressional Medal of Honor. In the words of the Medal of Honor citation, "By his undaunted courage, intrepid fighting spirit, and unwavering devotion to duty, Corporal Dunham gallantly gave his life for his country."[4]

Thomas Lickona, the author of several books including *Educating for Character* and *Character Matters*, explains that the premise of character education is that there are objectively good human qualities—virtues—that are enduring moral truths. Courage, fortitude, integrity, caring, citizenship, and trustworthiness are just a few examples. These moral truths transcend religious, cultural, and social differences and help us to distinguish right from wrong. They are rooted in our human nature. They tell us how we should act with other human beings to promote human dignity and build a well-functioning and civil society—a society in which everyone lives by the golden rule.[5]

To develop his or her character, a person must understand core virtues, care about them, and act upon them. This series of books aims to help young readers *want* to become people of character. The books will help young people understand such core ethical values as fairness, honesty, responsibility, respect, tolerance of others, fortitude, self-discipline, teamwork, and leadership. By offering examples of people today and notable figures in history who live and have lived these virtues, these books will inspire young readers to develop these traits in themselves.

Finally, through these books, young readers will see that if they act on these moral truths, they will make good choices.

They will be able to deal with frustration and anger, manage conflict resolution, overcome prejudice, handle peer pressure, and deal with bullying. The result, one hopes, will be middle schools, high schools, and neighborhoods in which young people care about one another and work with their classmates and neighbors to develop team spirit.

Character development is a lifelong task but an exciting challenge. The need for it has been with us since the beginning of civilization. As the ancient Greek philosopher Aristotle explained in his *Nicomachean Ethics*:

> The virtues we get by first exercising them . . . so too we become just by doing just acts, temperate by doing temperate acts, brave by doing brave acts. . . . Hence also it is no easy task to be good . . . to do this to the right person, to the right extent, at the right time, with the right motive, and in the right way, that is not easy; wherefore goodness is both rare and laudable and noble. . . . It makes no small difference, then, whether we form habits of one kind or of another from our very youth; it makes a very great difference, or rather all the difference.[6]

This development of one's character is truly *The Ultimate Gift* that we hope to give to our young people. In the movie version of Jim Stovall's book of the same name, a privileged young man receives a most unexpected inheritance from his grandfather. Instead of the sizeable inheritance of cash that he expects, the young man receives 12 tasks—or "gifts"—designed to challenge him on a journey of self-discovery. The gifts confront him with character choices that force him to decide how one can be truly happy. Is it the possession of money that brings us happiness, or is it what we do with the money that we have? Every one of us has been given gifts. Will we keep our gifts to ourselves, or will we share them with others?

Being a "person of character" can have multiple meanings. Psychologist Steven Pinker asks an interesting question in a

January 13, 2008, *New York Times Magazine* article titled "The Moral Instinct": "Which of the following people would you say is the most admirable: Mother Teresa, Bill Gates, or Norman Borlaug?" Pinker goes on to explain that although most people would say that, of course, Mother Teresa is the most admirable—a true person of character who ministered to the poor in Calcutta, was awarded the Noble Peace Prize, and was ranked in an American poll as the most admired person in the twentieth century—each of these three is a morally admirable person.

Pinker points out that Bill Gates made billions through his company Microsoft, but he also has decided to give away billions of dollars to help alleviate human misery in the United States and around the world. His charitable foundation is built on the principles that "All lives—no matter where they are being lived—have equal value" and "To whom much is given, much is expected."

Pinker notes that very few people have heard of Norman Borlaug, an agronomist who has spent his life developing high-yielding varieties of crops for third world countries. He is known as the "Father of the Green Revolution" because he used agricultural science to reduce world hunger and, by doing so, saved more than a billion lives. Borlaug is one of only five people in history to have won the Nobel Peace Prize, the Presidential Medal of Freedom, and the Congressional Gold Medal. He has devoted his long professional life and his scientific expertise to making the world a better place.

All of these people—although very different, from different places, and with different gifts—are people of character. They are, says Pinker, people with "a sixth sense, the moral sense." It is the sense of trying to do good in whatever situation one finds oneself.[7]

The authors and editors of the series *Character Education* hope that these books will help young readers discover their gifts and develop them, guided by a moral compass. "Do good and avoid evil." "Become all that you can be—a person of character." The books in this series teach these things and more. These books will correlate well with national social studies standards of learning. They will help teachers meet state standards for teaching social and emotional skills, as well as state guidelines for teaching ethics and character education.

Madonna M. Murphy, Ph.D.

Author of *Character Education in America's Blue Ribbon Schools* and professor of education, University of St. Francis, Joliet, Illinois

Sharon L. Banas, M.Ed.

Author of *Caring Messages for the School Year* and former values education coordinator and middle school social studies teacher, Sweet Home Central School District, Amherst and Tonawanda, New York

FOOTNOTES
1. William Kilpatrick. *Why Johnny Can't Tell Right from Wrong*, New York: Simon and Schuster, 1992.
2. Josephson Institute, 2006 *Josephson Institute Report Card on the Ethics of American Youth: Part One – Integrity.* Available online at: http://josephsoninstitute.org/pdf/ReportCard_press-release_2006-1013.pdf.
3. House Joint Resolution 366. May 11, 1994, 103rd Congress. 2d Session.
4. U.S. Army Center of Military History. *The Medal of Honor.* Available online at: www.history.army.mil/moh.html.
5. Thomas Lickona, *Educating for Character: Teaching Respect and Responsibility in the Schools.* New York: Bantam, 1991. Thomas Lickona, *Character Matters: How to Help Our Children Develop Good Judgment, Integrity, and Other Essential Virtues.* New York: Simon and Schuster Touchstone Books, 2004.
6. Richard McKeon, editor, "Nicomachean Ethics." *Basic Works of Aristotle,* Chicago: Random House, Clarendon Press, 1941.
7. Steven Pinker, "The Moral Instinct," *The New York Times,* January 13, 2008. Available online at www.newyorktimes.com.

BEING A
RESPONSIBLE
PERSON

The buck stops here.

—sign on the desk of
U.S. President Harry S. Truman (1884–1972)

To be responsible means to be answerable or accountable. A responsible person can be relied upon to make a strong effort to perform his or her duties and to honor commitments. If a person acts responsibly, others know that this person is dependable.

In David Isaacs's 2001 book, *Character Building*, he makes a distinction between just meeting responsibilities and being a responsible person. An individual can meet obligations partway while complaining and arguing about it, but this does not make him or her responsible. On the other hand, a responsible person will fulfill obligations to the best of his or her ability.

Isaacs explains that a person must make responsible decisions and be responsible for his or her actions. "A responsible human being accepts the consequences of his own actions, intentional or not . . . ," says Isaacs. For example, if you decide to throw a hot sauce packet across the cafeteria to your friend and it hits her in the eye, you should apologize and take her to the nurse if she is hurt. You didn't hit her in the eye on purpose, but you should take responsibility for your action and try to "undo the harm," explains Isaacs.

A person can learn to be responsible. Samuel P. Oliner and Pearl Oliner explored that question in their book, *The*

The woman pictured in *The Responsible Woman* is seen soaring to new heights because she is able to manage her many responsibilities so well. Separately, artist James Christensen also painted *The Burdens of the Responsible Man*, based on his mixed feelings about his own responsibilities. (*The Responsible Woman by James C. Christensen, © James C. Christensen, used by permission from The Greenwich Workshop®, Inc.*)

Altruistic Personality: Rescuers of Jews in Nazi Europe, which is about non-Jewish people who rescued Jews from the Nazis during World War II. The authors discovered that these rescuers had parents who acted as models of responsible behavior. Parents teach responsibility by example. Parents also set standards of responsibility they expect their children to follow. The Oliners explained, "Adults whose behaviors are consistently and dependably responsible communicate the message that such behaviors are self-rewarding, making children more likely to internalize standards of responsibility, caring, and dependability and to adopt them as their own."

Artist James Christensen created an image of just such a responsible person. In 1992, he painted *The Responsible Woman* in honor of his wife, Carole. In the painting, a woman is surrounded by symbols that represent her many responsibilities. She cares for a baby and a dog. She cooks, cleans, and sews. In addition, there is a clock, a diary, and a compass, which symbolize her role as time and history keeper and navigator for the family. With all of her responsibilities well met, the woman is able to literally reach new heights as she is shown soaring above the treetops.

Everyone has responsibilities, just as the subject of *The Responsible Woman* does. A student has responsibilities at school, in sports, and as a member of clubs. If you have a job, such as babysitting, you demonstrate responsible behavior there, as well. Beyond these everyday personal responsibilities, you can choose to be responsible for others through charitable outreach and social activism.

LIVING A RESPONSIBLE LIFE

Louis Caldera is an example of someone who has tried to live responsibly in many areas of his life. Caldera was born to Mexican immigrant parents in El Paso, Texas. When he was five years old, his family moved to the public housing complex Boyle Heights in East Los Angeles. Later, they moved to Whittier, California. Caldera was the oldest boy of his parents' five children. From an early age, he had an appreciation for how hard his parents worked to care for their family, and he took on a variety of jobs to lend a hand. "I knew my family was poor and, at times, struggled to put

TAKING RESPONSIBILITY THROUGH AMERICORPS

The Corporation for National and Community Service is the country's largest grant maker, which means it gives money to charitable organizations. The corporation offers money to support service and volunteering. One of its programs, called AmeriCorps, boasts more than 70,000 volunteers each year. People who are at least 17 years old and are U.S. citizens, U.S. nationals, or lawful permanent residents can join AmeriCorps. The volunteer opportunities that AmeriCorps State and AmeriCorps National offer are varied and include everything from cleaning parks to tutoring to building homes.

AmeriCorps VISTA gives volunteers a chance to specifically help fight poverty. Those who join AmeriCorps VISTA commit to a year of full-time service. AmeriCorps National Civilian Community Corps accepts volunteers between the ages of 18 and 24 who are willing to give 10 months of full-time work. These volunteers live at one of four campuses across the country and work together on team projects.

AmeriCorps volunteers gain satisfaction through their work for others. In addition, once their commitment is completed, they earn money toward a college education or to pay off certain student loans. Alternatively, if you want to volunteer outside the United States, the Peace Corps might be the organization for you. Since its start in 1960, the Peace Corps has had 190,000 volunteers serve in 139 different countries. Peace Corps volunteers help address many issues, including education, health, and the environment.

food on the table," said Caldera. "I felt I had to step up to the plate."

In California, Caldera's father learned to style hair and opened a hair salon in a strip mall. The owner of the mall offered to lower his rent if he would take on the added responsibility of keeping the parking lot clean. At only 10 years old, Caldera would travel to the mall three days a week at 4 A.M. to help his family clean the lot. For two to three hours, Caldera would clean the parking lot with an industrial vacuum cleaner, empty trash cans, and pick up litter by hand. Then, he would return home and prepare for his day at school. "I did this for two years, but the lessons I learned have lasted a lifetime. I acquired discipline and a strong work ethic, and learned at an early age the importance of balancing life's competing interests—in my case school, homework, and a job," Caldera told *Reader's Digest* in 2001.

As a high school student, Caldera juggled college preparatory classes and a full-time job at a fast food restaurant. Whatever money he earned, he gave directly to his mother to benefit the family. Caldera was also a dedicated student. "My parents sacrificed a lot to help us have a better life," he said. "I felt responsible to do well in school to acknowledge their sacrifice."

By age 10, Caldera was already dreaming of one day entering public life. He had been inspired by politicians John F. Kennedy and Robert Kennedy's lifelong commitment to public service. Like the Kennedy brothers, Caldera wanted to address society's concerns, especially poverty. To pursue his dream, Caldera knew that he needed to excel academically so that he could earn a full scholarship to college. He met his goal: Caldera was accepted to and graduated from the United States Military Academy at West Point. After graduation, he served the country for an additional five years in the U.S. Army's military police. Caldera then attended Harvard University, where he earned a law degree from Harvard Law

Louis Caldera (seen with Chicago High School student Zaynab Kamal in 2000 during the Army's Multicultural Leadership Conference) has worked at managing tough responsibilities since he was a child and encourages others to reach their goals and meet their responsibilities.

School and a degree of Master in Business Administration from Harvard Business School.

After graduate school, Caldera worked with the law firm O'Melveny and Myers in Los Angeles. The law office's high-rise building could be seen by the people of Boyle Heights, his family's old neighborhood. It was a daily reminder to Caldera of his goal to help the disadvantaged. In 1992, he was elected to the California State Assembly, where he represented those in the Boyle Heights area, as well as a section of downtown Los Angeles. During his five years as assemblyman, Caldera championed the formation of charter schools and raised the academic standards of all the schools in his district. "I have always believed in education; it made such a difference in my life. I wanted to give other young people the opportunity," said Caldera. He also increased job opportunities and improved neighborhood conditions in the areas he represented.

President Bill Clinton named Caldera the managing director and chief operating officer of the Corporation for National and Community Service, which is the organization that sponsors AmeriCorps. This job was a good fit for Caldera because he is an advocate of volunteering and charitable outreach, especially among young people. "We who have resources should use them for the good of others," Caldera said. He explained that those resources could be financial, intellectual, or any talent one has to share.

In 1998, President Clinton appointed Caldera the secretary of the U.S. Army, and he served in this position until 2001. During his term, he was responsible for increasing the Army's budget, supplying equipment for the troops, and helping transfer control of the Panama Canal from the United States to Panama. He has said he is especially proud of the educational plan he developed for the troops. Caldera began a program in which soldiers could complete further education online, whether it was a college degree or certificate training.

From 2003 until 2006, Caldera was the president of the University of New Mexico and then became a professor at the university's law school. Caldera taught until President Barack Obama appointed him as director of the White House Military Office at the start of his term on January 20, 2009. In this position, Caldera coordinated military support for the White House, including presidential travel.

In his new role, Caldera approved a misguided mission for which he would take responsibility. On April 27, 2009, one of the president's 747 airplanes, known as Air Force One when the president is aboard, and an F-16 fighter aircraft flew at 1,000 feet over New York City. The purpose of the low-flying flight was to obtain patriotic photographs of the president's plane flying over the Statue of Liberty.

Although some law enforcement officials were told of the mission in advance, the public had not been informed

HELPING THE PRESIDENT MANAGE RESPONSIBILITIES

The U.S. president's cabinet is filled with advisors who share their expertise with him. The U.S. Constitution allows for the formation of a cabinet so, it says, the president can seek "the opinion, in writing, of the principal officer in each of the executive departments, upon any subject relating to the duties of their respective offices." However, the Constitution does not say exactly how many cabinet members there should be, or which executive departments should be represented. George Washington only chose four cabinet members: Secretary of State Thomas Jefferson, Secretary of the Treasury Alexander Hamilton, Attorney General Edmund Randolph, and Secretary of War Henry Knox.

In contrast, as of 2009, the presidential cabinet includes the vice president and 15 heads of executive departments, including agriculture, education, energy, health and human services, homeland security, and housing and urban development. The four positions considered most powerful are those that Washington had when he was president: the secretaries of state, treasury, and defense, and the attorney general.

The president nominates a cabinet member, and the U.S. Senate must confirm that individual through a simple majority, which means that more than 50 percent of the senators must agree to appoint that person to the cabinet. The Constitution prohibits a member of either house of Congress from being a cabinet member. In this way, the executive and legislative branches remain separate. In addition, no cabinet member can be related to the president. This law came into effect as a reaction to President John F. Kennedy appointing his brother Robert as his attorney general.

beforehand. The sight of the 747 and the fighter jet alarmed some people because it reminded them of the September 11, 2001 terrorist attack on the World Trade Center, which was very close to the lower Manhattan location of the flyover.

Interestingly, cabinet members are in line of succession for the presidency, which means they are part of a line of people who will take over the presidency if something happens to the president. If, for example, the president dies while in office, the next in line to take over is the vice president. If something also happened to the vice president, the presidency would fall to the speaker of the house, followed by the president pro tempore of the Senate, and then to the cabinet members. Sometimes, all of the people in this line of succession must be present for important government events, such as the State of the Union Address. As a safeguard, one cabinet member does not attend and is kept in a secure, secret location. This person is known as the designated survivor because if something tragic happens at the event, he or she will still be alive and can immediately assume the presidency.

The secretary of the army is the head of the Department of the Army. Louis Caldera, discussed earlier, held this position. The job includes making decisions about everything involving the U.S. Army, from employees to equipment to finances. Even though the title includes the word *secretary*, this person is not a member of the cabinet. The secretary of the army reports to the secretary of defense, who is a cabinet member, and to the president.

The candidate for secretary of the army is nominated by the president and is confirmed by the U.S. Senate. This person must be a civilian, which means someone who is not a member of the military, and must have been separated from any military service for at least five years. This requirement is part of the system of checks and balances in the U.S. government. It assures that the military doesn't have too much power in the government.

Media reports noted that some people who saw the 747 followed by the fighter jet evacuated their buildings and called 911 to report the incident. When Caldera learned of the panic caused by the mission, he released a statement taking responsibility for the flight.

New York City Mayor Michael Bloomberg and President Obama requested a full investigation into the origins of the mission to discover why the flight was approved, and especially why the public wasn't informed in advance. The White House Counsel's Office compiled a report that detailed a series of miscommunications between Caldera and his deputy director regarding the planning and approval of the mission. The report concluded that clearer procedures governing the use of Air Force One for special missions other than presidential travel must be put in place. On May 8, 2009, Caldera took responsibility for the incident and resigned his White House position. In a statement, Caldera said he resigned so the concerns about the flyover would no longer be a "distraction to the important work [Obama was] doing as president."

Caldera continues to look for ways to contribute to society. "I still believe in public service," he said, "and I look forward to whatever the next opportunity will be."

THE PROFESSOR'S LAST LESSON

In 2006, Randy Pausch, a professor at Carnegie Mellon University and the father of three young children, was diagnosed with a serious form of cancer called pancreatic cancer. His life is a terrific example of perseverance and of responsibility to family, work, and society.

Pausch fought the disease bravely because he felt a strong sense of responsibility to his children and his wife and wanted to stay alive to be with them. He underwent a major operation that removed the pancreatic tumor, his gallbladder, a third of his pancreas, a third of his stomach, and a large portion of his small intestine. He also had to endure the exhaustion and other side-effects of numerous chemotherapy treatments. "I signed up for the hardest treatments that could be thrown at me because I wanted to be around as long as possible to be there for my kids," wrote Pausch in his book, *The Last Lecture*. Tragically, the cancer spread to his liver, and doctors said he would die from the disease.

The Last Lecture is based upon a last lecture Pausch gave to his students at Carnegie Mellon University. The lecture included the vital lessons in his life that he wanted to teach to his students. In the presentation, he talked about the importance of setting goals in your life and pursuing them no matter what blocks the way. Pausch shared his own childhood dreams and the obstacles he overcame to fulfill them. For example, as a child he wanted to float in zero gravity. As a professor, he and his students designed a virtual reality

Professor Randy Pausch shared his life lessons with the world while he fought a brave battle with cancer. Above, Pausch, who had pancreatic cancer, carries his wife, Jai, back to her seat after speaking at Carnegie Mellon University's May 2008 graduation ceremony.

experiment to be used aboard NASA's special antigravity plane. Pausch thought this would be his chance to experience weightlessness, but he discovered that professors couldn't accompany the students aboard the plane. Pausch believed that obstacles—or "brick walls," as he called them—could be overcome. "The brick walls are there for a reason," he said. "They're not there to keep us out. The brick walls are there to give us a chance to show how much we want something." He did some research and found that local journalists covering the flight would be welcomed on board. He resigned as faculty advisor and applied to go as a journalist. He was accepted and had his chance to float.

Pausch had another childhood dream: He visited Disneyland when he was eight years old, and from that moment on, he hoped to design rides for the Walt Disney Company. In 1989, after he earned his Ph.D. in computer science from Carnegie Mellon University, he sent an application letter to Disney to become an "Imagineer"—a person who creates Disney rides. The company quickly rejected him. He joined the faculty at the University of Virginia and worked diligently in the field of virtual reality. Seven years later, he heard that Disney was building a virtual reality ride based on the film *Aladdin*. He contacted the company and set up a meeting with Jon Snoddy, the man in charge of the Aladdin project. Snoddy agreed to allow Pausch to join his team during Pausch's leave of absence from his university job. Pausch lived his dream of becoming a Disney Imagineer.

An important point that Pausch makes about fulfilling childhood dreams is this: There needs to be much hard work and skill-building to support the dreams. One of his students realized the dream of working on *Star Wars* films. "They didn't hire him for his dreams," Pausch said about this student. "They hired him for his skills."

In the last months of his life, Professor Pausch continued to battle his cancer with chemotherapy. He decided to testify before Congress, even though he was physically weak. He told the government that there needed to be more funding for pancreatic cancer research. He realized that the increase in funding would not improve his own chances to live, but he felt a responsibility to make a difference for those who would suffer from pancreatic cancer in the future. Pausch died on July 25, 2008, at the age of 47. Even with his many accomplishments, what was most important to him was the time he spent with his family.

2 QUALITIES OF A RESPONSIBLE PERSON

When we do the best we can, we never know what miracle is wrought in our life, or in the life of another.

—Helen Keller (1880–1968),
American author and activist

Certain qualities are necessary for becoming a responsible person. The first is the ability to set realistic goals. "Set realistic goals that are in concert with your strengths," advises New York-based school psychologist Jennifer Obrizok. Take a truthful look at your interests and abilities when you decide upon your goals. For example, if you have a passion for football, but you are very small, you probably won't be a star tackle in the NFL. However, if you are also good at teaching others, you might make a terrific football coach or physical education teacher.

In addition to being realistic, the goals you set should be challenging to you. Also, make sure that your goals are just that—*your* goals. "You need to decide what you want to be and not what those around you want you to be," explains

Nancy Kelly, a licensed clinical social worker in Pleasant Valley, New York.

Once you've settled on a realistic goal, you have to be diligent in pursuit of that goal. *Diligence* means "giving an energetic effort, working hard, and doing your best." Self-discipline is another vital quality that goes along with diligence. *Self-discipline* means "regulating yourself or exercising control over your actions." Let's say you've decided to become a concert violinist, which will require you to be diligent with your music lessons. You also need to practice one hour every day, but sitting and watching television instead certainly seems like a good way to pass time. That is where the self-discipline comes into play: Walk away from the screen and pick up the bow.

Perseverance is another key part of being responsible. You are bound to run into barriers to your goals. Perseverance is the ability to continue toward a goal despite obstacles. "You have to expect failure at some point," Kelly says. "Figure out what you can learn from the failure and move on." A quality that goes hand in hand with perseverance is optimism. An optimistic person keeps a positive attitude and feels that things will work out well. A person with an optimistic outlook is more likely to persevere than to give up. Finally, flexibility—the ability to adapt to change—is also important. "Have a backup plan," Obrizok advises.

HELEN KELLER AND ANNE SULLIVAN

Both Helen Keller and her teacher and friend, Anne Sullivan, set realistic yet challenging goals for themselves. They possessed the same qualities as other people who are considered to be responsible: diligence, self-discipline, perseverance, optimism, and flexibility.

Helen Keller was born in Tuscumbia, Alabama, on June 27, 1880. When Helen was younger than two years old, she suffered a high fever that almost killed her. The illness left her deaf and blind. Suddenly, she had lost the ability to communicate easily with her family. She acted out in frustration. One time, she dumped her baby sister, Mildred, from a doll cradle. Fortunately, Helen's mother was there to catch the infant before she fell to the floor. Helen was ill mannered. She would race around the dining room, stealing and eating food from others' plates. Captain and Mrs. Keller knew Helen needed help. Alexander Graham Bell, the inventor who also taught deaf students, put the Keller family in contact with Michael Anagnos, the director of Perkins School for the Blind in Boston, Massachusetts. Anagnos sent Anne Sullivan to be Helen's teacher.

Sullivan was 21 years old when she arrived at the Kellers' home on March 3, 1887. Soon after her arrival, Helen threw a temper tantrum and knocked out Sullivan's front teeth. Sullivan felt it would be easier to teach Helen if the two could be alone. They moved together to a small cottage on the Kellers' property. There, Sullivan diligently taught Helen to fingerspell using the manual alphabet. This is the same alphabet used to communicate with deaf individuals, but Sullivan formed the letters in Helen's hand so she could feel their shape.

Helen had been able to speak a few words, such as *wa-wa* for "water," before she lost her vision and hearing. However, she could not make the connection between the words Sullivan spelled and the objects the words represented. One day, Sullivan took Helen out to the water pump, where the water spilled out of a mug and over Helen's hand. Sullivan spelled *w-a-t-e-r* over and over until Helen joyously understood. One of the words Helen had spoken as a toddler had been the very one to unlock her world of isolation.

From that time, Helen became an enthusiastic student. Despite living in darkness and silence, she learned to fingerspell, write, and read braille. In May of 1888, Sullivan took Helen to the Perkins School for a visit. Following that, Helen studied at the school each winter. She heard about a deaf-blind girl, Ragnhild Kaata of Norway, who had learned to

Helen Keller (*left*) and her teacher Anne Sullivan set difficult goals and achieved them with hard work and patience. Here, 12-year-old Keller reads Sullivan's sign language with her hands.

speak. Helen was determined to learn to speak, as well. She went to the Horace Mann School in Boston, where a teacher worked with her. Helen learned to form words after only 11 lessons, but it took long hours of study with Sullivan to make Helen's spoken words understandable.

KEVIN EVERETT: MIRACLE MAN

In the book, *Standing Tall: The Kevin Everett Story*, author Sam Carchidi tells the tale of professional football player Kevin Everett's devastating spinal injury and his miraculous recovery. Everett was a tight end for the Buffalo Bills. On September 9, 2007, he tackled Denver Broncos player Domenik Hixon. Everett's head was a bit too low during the tackle, and he was badly hurt. He fell to the ground and couldn't feel his arms or legs. He couldn't even offer the fans a reassuring thumbs-up gesture.

The medical team carefully made certain that his neck and spine wouldn't accidentally move and placed him in the ambulance. They gave him a drug to reduce spinal cord swelling and iced saline to cause a mild hypothermia—a lowered body temperature. They hoped the lowered body temperature would keep the spinal cord from swelling and slow the formation of toxic substances that might worsen the injury.

Everett underwent spinal surgery at Millard Fillmore Gates Circle Hospital in Buffalo, New York. After the surgery, surgeon Andrew Cappuccino told the media that Everett's injuries could be life threatening. He said that Everett only had a 5 to 10 percent chance of a full neurological recovery. The next day, however, Dr. Cappuccino was able to report that Everett had movement in his arms and legs.

That news was encouraging, but Everett had long hours of grueling recovery work ahead. Luckily, he had the constant support of his mother, Patricia Dugas, and his fiancée, Wiande Moore. They stayed by his side day and night. He also had a skilled team of medical and rehabilitation specialists to help him.

In 1892, young Helen wrote a story called "The Frost King" that she sent to Anagnos, the Perkins School's director. He was so pleased with it that he printed the piece in a Perkins publication. People noticed that the story was extremely similar to author Margaret Canby's story "The

Less than two weeks after his accident, Everett was transferred to Memorial Hermann TIRR, a rehabilitation hospital in Houston, Texas. At first, he couldn't sit or even hold a spoon. Everett worked with different therapists who helped him to sit, stand, and feed himself. During rehabilitation, Everett said other patients inspired him to keep trying. One patient in particular, Virgil Calhoun, encouraged Everett with some friendly competition. He would tell Everett how many miles he had walked on the treadmill or how much weight he had lifted and challenge Everett to beat him. One month after Everett suffered his spinal injury, he took his first steps. "I knew I would eventually get to this point, that it was just a matter of time, just a matter of hard work," said Everett.

Everett knew all about hard work. After graduating from high school, Everett dreamed of attending the University of Miami in Florida. Unfortunately, his grades weren't high enough. He went to Kilgore College, a junior college, to better his grades and soon earned a spot at the University of Miami. Coach Mario Cristobal at the university remembered how diligent Everett was about improving his football skills. He would arrive early for practices and spend extra time in the weight room and studying game films.

Everett's doctors do not think he'll ever play football again, and he feels saddened that his football playing days are behind him. However, Everett is looking forward to his future. He plans to marry and start a large family. Then, perhaps, he said, he will coach football, buy a restaurant, or become an inspirational speaker.

Frost Fairies." Helen was accused of copying the story and calling it her own, and Anagnos questioned her at length about her previous knowledge of Canby's story. Helen felt that the director did not believe in her innocence, and she lost him as a friend.

Finally, Helen discovered that three years earlier an adult friend may have read the Canby story to her, but she did not remember this. Even Margaret Canby did not believe that Helen had intended to plagiarize the story. Still, after this, Helen found it difficult to regain confidence about her writing ability. She was often worried that her writing did not come from her own imagination, but that she had heard or read the idea somewhere. But she persisted and completed many articles, books, and speeches during her lifetime.

Helen decided that she wanted to attend Radcliffe College in Cambridge, Massachusetts. Agnes Irwin, the dean of Radcliffe, did not think that Helen should attend the school and advised her to consider other colleges. Helen was unwavering. She studied for two years at Wright-Humason School for the Deaf in New York City and then at Cambridge School for Young Ladies in Massachusetts. In June of 1899, she took the entrance exam for Radcliffe and passed. She graduated with honors from Radcliffe in 1904 as the first deaf-blind person to graduate college in the United States.

As an adult, Keller became a world-famous author and lecturer. She traveled throughout the United States and the world to support the causes of blind and deaf individuals. She spoke about the right of the disabled to be educated and to work, and championed the rights of women and the poor. Keller worked as ambassador for the American Foundation for the Blind. She even starred in a documentary about her life, for which she won an Academy Award in 1955. Four years before her death in 1968, Keller was awarded the Presidential Medal of Freedom, the highest honor given to a civilian.

Alexander Graham Bell (*right*) put Helen Keller's family in touch with the responsible and hard-working Anne Sulllivan (*middle*), who would go on to change Helen's life. Here, the three communicate in Chautauqua, New York, using sign language. Bell fingerspells into Keller's right hand, while she uses her left hand to read Sullivan's lips.

SULLIVAN'S DIFFICULT, AMAZING LIFE

Anne Sullivan is often thought of as the talented, determined teacher who wouldn't give up on Keller, but she had a challenging life, as well. At age 7, young Anne suffered from trachoma, a bacterial infection that left her nearly blind. Her mother died, and two years later, she and her brother, Jimmie, were placed in the Almshouse in Tewksbury, Massachusetts. Life at the home for the poor was difficult. The workers were abusive and the residents were often ill. Jimmie became sick and died there three months after they arrived.

Anne was determined to escape the poorhouse and receive an education. One day, Frank B. Sanborn, an official for the State Board of Charities, was inspecting the facility. She approached him and begged him to allow her to attend school. He agreed and sent her to the Perkins Institute for the Blind. At age 15, Anne underwent eye operations, which restored some of her sight. Even so, throughout her life, her eyes often hurt and she would become nauseous after long periods of reading. Anne studied diligently while at Perkins and graduated as valedictorian of her class. While at the school, Anne met a deaf-blind student named Laura Bridgman, and she learned to fingerspell in order to communicate with her. When the Keller family requested a teacher for Helen, Anne's academic skills together with her knowledge of fingerspelling made her an excellent choice.

Sullivan, now an adult of 21, was the perfect teacher for young Helen. She refused to give up, even after Helen knocked out her teeth. She persisted in fingerspelling until Helen made the connection between what was being spelled and the object it represented. If Sullivan had quit, Helen might never have broken free from her silent world.

As you marvel at Helen's hard work at school, realize that Sullivan attended every class with her to fingerspell the professors' lectures into her hand. Also, many of the textbooks

MELVIN JUETTE: PERSEVERANCE DEFINED

Melvin Juette was a gang member in Chicago. At just 16 years old, he was shot in a gang-related incident. The bullet hit his lower spine, and he was paralyzed.

While Juette was in the hospital, he decided that he was going to face his injury with an optimistic attitude. He remembered a boy from his childhood who had suffered from muscular dystrophy and was confined to a wheelchair. Juette recalled that the boy was pessimistic, which was difficult for those around him. Juette was determined not to end up like that kid.

While at the Rehabilitation Institute of Chicago for his therapy, Juette joined the rehabilitation center's junior wheelchair basketball team. The coach loaned him a lightweight

After becoming a paraplegic, Melvin Juette (*right*) was able to be successful in college and basketball. Above, Juette is awarded a Chicago State University pin from the interim university president Dr. Frank Pogue on Disability Awareness Day on April 15, 2009.

sports wheelchair to use for three months until his family could buy him one. Eventually, he was recruited to play wheelchair basketball for the University of Wisconsin-Whitewater.

(continues)

(continued)

At first, Juette had trouble with his college classes. A counselor at the school taught him study skills and time management skills, so he could study more efficiently. Juette worked diligently in his courses and succeeded.

In 1991, his wheelchair basketball team competed in the college championships. Juette's playing ability was so impressive that he was invited to try out for the U.S. national team that would play in the 1994 Paralympics. He didn't make it that year, but he practiced and trained harder. Juette liked to quote Jack Reid, Diamond Director in the Amway Corporation, who said, "Good things come to those who wait, but here's a rule that's slicker. It's what you do while you wait that gets you there much quicker."

Juette tried out for the national team again in 1994 and made it. He went on to win two gold and two bronze medals in the Gold Cup international competitions. He also helped form and was a player on the National Wheelchair Basketball Association Milwaukee Bucks.

When Juette reflects on the shooting that cost him the use of his legs, he considers it the worst and best thing that could have happened to him. If it were not for the accident, he would not have attended college or gone on to a successful basketball career. Instead, he fears he might have continued in the gang and been jailed or killed.

were not available in braille, so Sullivan stayed up late into the night to read them and fingerspell the words for Helen.

When Helen wrote books and articles, Sullivan helped her research and edit them. In a letter excerpt quoted on the American Foundation for the Blind's Web site, Sullivan wrote, ". . . whatever Helen writes represents my labor as well as hers. The genius is hers, but much of the drudgery is mine."

Sullivan accompanied Helen on her lecture tours around the world. When money was tight, they even performed a stage act together to entertain audiences and earn money.

Sullivan was presented with the Teacher's Medal at the Panama-Pacific International Exposition in San Francisco in honor of her superb teaching skills.

BEATING LUPUS

Many non-famous people have also found ways to lead responsible lives. Aiden Gallagher, an 11-year-old from Salt Point, New York, was an excellent student and athlete involved in soccer, softball, and Irish step dancing. Then, something went terribly wrong. Aiden suffered horrible fatigue, headaches, and arthritis pain. One night, she awoke with terrible stomach pains. "I thought I was being stabbed in the stomach by 12 knives," Aiden said.

Aiden's doctor diagnosed her with systemic lupus erythematosus. This is an autoimmune disease in which the body produces antibodies that attack its own skin, joints, and organs. Lupus has no known cause, and a cure has yet to be discovered. To treat the disease, Aiden's doctor prescribed medicine, but the lupus did not improve. She had to be admitted to the hospital every few weeks to undergo chemotherapy treatments, which left her exhausted and nauseated.

At the same time as Aiden was fighting to save her life, she was fighting to keep her life as full and rich as possible. "I would not let the disease take away everything that was important to me," she explained. The lupus symptoms and the medical treatments made it difficult for her to attend school. On many days, she pushed herself to classes and studied hard. At other times, a tutor came to her house to help her keep up with her classwork. Aiden's hard work was rewarded when she was chosen for the Junior National Honor Society in middle school.

Unfortunately, Aiden had to give up soccer and Irish step dance, but she refused to quit a season of softball. She loved the sport and didn't want to let her teammates down. However, playing softball wasn't easy for her. Aiden was the catcher for her team, and it was difficult to squat and stand

As Aiden Gallagher lives with the autoimmune connective tissue disease lupus, she continues to spread the word about the disease and raise money to find a cure. People with lupus are often in pain as their immune system attacks the body's cells and tissue, which results in inflammation and tissue damage.

with her arthritic knees. In addition, lupus often worsens with sun exposure, so Aiden had to wear long-sleeved shirts and wide-brimmed hats during practice and games—even in scorching heat.

Aiden kept a positive attitude about her disease and reached out to help others who were suffering. "I think that I was diagnosed with lupus for a reason," she said. "Maybe that reason is to go and spread the word about the disease." Aiden and her friend Una-Marie Antczak, another young lupus patient, suggested that the Lupus Foundation of America sell purple armbands to raise money and awareness, similar to Lance Armstrong's yellow LIVESTRONG armbands. The Lupus Foundation agreed, and as of late 2008, sales of the purple lupus armbands had raised $330,000. Aiden even acts as teen spokesperson for the Lupus Foundation of America in its 2007 public service video.

Aiden has also begun her own charity organization, Beating Lupus. The organization hand beads and sells purple Swarovski crystal bracelets to raise funds for lupus education and research. Through a branch of her charity, Comforts for Chemo, Aiden also distributes handmade quilts and Moshi pillows to first-time chemotherapy patients.

In 2009, Aiden celebrated her 16th birthday. Instead of dreaming about presents for herself, she planned a magical Sweet 16 dinner dance to raise money for her charity. The event raised $16,000.

BEING RESPONSIBLE AT SCHOOL AND HOME

If one advances confidently in the direction of his dreams and endeavors to live the life which he has imagined, he will meet with a success unexpected in common hours.

—Henry David Thoreau (1817–1862),
American author and philosopher

Nine-year-old Lin Hao of China took his school responsibilities to a heroic level. On May 12, 2008, a 7.9 magnitude earthquake hit the Sichuan province of China, killing nearly 70,000 people. Lin Hao was at school in Wenchuan County, which was at the exact center of the region where the earthquake hit. His classroom collapsed around him. He suffered head and arm injuries as a result, but that didn't stop him from rescuing two of his classmates from the rubble. When asked what motivated him to save his peers,

Lin Hao said, "I was hall monitor; it was my job to look after my classmates."

Every day, you are called upon to meet responsibilities, as well. It is possible to do it all and do it well. In the beginning of the day, you may go to school and study hard. "[For kids], school is a job, and you need to do schoolwork to the best of your ability," explains school psychologist Jennifer Obrizok. You have a responsibility to attend class, be respectful and pay attention to the teacher, and complete the classwork using your best effort. Obrizok also says that a student has a social responsibility to fulfill by being kind to and helping other students.

After school, you might participate in sports or clubs, and you should give your full effort there. A responsible participant in sports goes to practices and games because teammates are depending on him or her. People active in sports should keep trying to improve sports skills and strive for excellent performance, and they should also encourage teammates and help them perfect their skills. These same ideas hold true for any after-school clubs or activities. It is important, however, to try not to overload yourself with too many extracurricular activities. Choose the ones that are most important to you and say no to others. "It is better to excel in certain activities and not to do everything in a mediocre [so-so] way," says Obrizok.

After sports or extracurricular activities, you go home to do chores, finish homework, and maybe take care of your pets. Homework is given to reinforce lessons learned in school, as well as to gain new knowledge and skills. Obrizok notes that a responsible student would set aside a certain amount of time for homework each school day. She suggests a student might consider staying after school to finish homework, so he or she has access to library resources and teachers if extra help is needed.

Professional organizer Ellen Kutner says that it is important to choose a particular space for homework. She suggests that a student should have an area with good lighting, a desk with a lot of room, and a comfortable chair. The study area should be free of electronic distractions, such as cell phones and televisions, so the student can concentrate. It is best to tackle one assignment at a time. "The new thing is single tasking—doing one thing from beginning to end," says Kutner. "Multitasking is less productive."

When a teacher gives you large homework projects, such as research papers, it is easier to break the assignment down into small, manageable parts, advises Obrizok. You might set aside a week for library and Internet research, a week to write the paper, and a few days for editing. Don't forget to

HOW TO APPROACH A TEACHER

You studied hard for a test, and you were shocked to receive a poor grade. Gather your confidence and talk to the teacher about the exam. Even if you believe the teacher made some errors, approach him or her calmly. Psychologist Jennifer Obrizok suggests that students "ask, 'Could we review the test together?' Then, point out the mistakes politely." A teacher is a human being, complete with all the normal human responses. If you speak angrily, the teacher might defend his or her original decision instead of being open to considering your arguments.

On the other hand, if you simply don't understand where you went wrong on the test, the teacher will want to help you. Remember, you are both on the same side: You want to learn and the teacher wants you to learn. "Part of being a responsible person is asking for help when you don't understand," says Obrizok. "You are not going to know everything." To get help, you may ask if there is a convenient time to schedule an extra help session or say, "Can you tell me where I can improve?" If you are worried about your grades, you may even request extra-credit work.

allow a bit of extra time in case something goes wrong, such as running out of printer ink or coming down with a cold. This way, the project doesn't seem overwhelming. In addition, this strategy helps to avoid procrastination. If you wait until the last minute, stress increases, and the project doesn't reflect your finest work.

If you have a big test coming up, you could decide to read and take notes on a certain number of pages or chapters each night. "Write down your notes; don't just highlight," advises Obrizok. The act of writing helps your mind absorb the information more effectively.

MANAGING TIME AND SPACE

As a man with a terminal illness, Randy Pausch, author of *The Last Lecture*, had an insightful view on the irreplaceable nature of time. "Time is all you have. You may find, one day, that you have less of it than you think," he explained in his book. A responsible person understands the value of time and uses time effectively. This person sets short-term goals, such as making the honor roll. A responsible person also sets long-term goals, such as what type of job he or she wants to have as an adult. Then, this person works diligently to accomplish his or her goals.

In a lecture Pausch gave about time management, he offered some concrete advice about using the gift of time wisely. He said to choose to spend your time doing something that inspires you, about which you are passionate, and that you enjoy. "If you're not going to have fun, why do it?" asked Pausch. In addition, make sure you are using your time meaningfully. "Don't do the wrong things wonderfully," Pausch advised. "Don't polish the underside of the banister well."

Pausch suggested keeping a time journal. In the journal, write down exactly how you use your time, just as you might keep track of the money you spend. Then, you can evaluate whether you spend too much time playing Guitar Hero or texting friends, and make a change.

Kutner says that a paper or electronic planner could be a useful time management tool. Many planners include a monthly calendar in which you can record an overview of your upcoming obligations and events, such as exams, small jobs, and birthday celebrations. The planner will also have weekly and daily sections to include further detailed information, such as: Math test on the Pythagorean theorem on Friday. In addition to using a planner, Kutner suggested writing a daily "to do" list and posting it in a highly visible place. Decide which things are most important and set these

LIMITING SCREEN TIME

In *The Last Lecture*, author Randy Pausch called television "mankind's greatest time waster." This opinion came from an individual with terminal cancer, who knew just how precious time is. Did you know that if you spend two hours per day in front of a TV or computer over a 75-year time period, you will have used six and a half years of your life this way?

Not surprisingly, spending too much time in front of the television or computer can affect other elements in your life. A study by Iman Sharif and James D. Sargent, published in the journal *Pediatrics*, concluded that increased television screen time during the week was linked with poorer performance at school.

Too much screen time is also linked to obesity. The American Academy of Pediatrics (AAP) recommends that young people limit their screen time to two hours a day. In addition, the organization suggests that boys walk 11,000 steps a day and girls walk 13,000 steps a day. Kelly Laurson and his colleagues at Iowa State University and the National Institute on Media and the Family studied 709 children between ages 7 and 12. The children wore pedometers and answered priorities by giving each item on the list a number, with the most urgent being number one.

Another way to add time to your busy schedule is to organize your space. That way, you don't waste time searching for things. Kutner suggests sorting through school paperwork at the end of each year. Throw away or recycle what you won't need next semester. If you choose to keep report cards and other interesting or important papers, place them in a small bin or a folder. However, the next time you add paperwork to this pile, reconsider what you kept last time. "Set boundaries and limits," says Kutner. "Next year, don't just buy another bin."

questionnaires about the time they spent in front of a television or computer screen. Then, their bodies were measured to check for obesity. More than half the children didn't meet the AAP recommendations for steps or screen time, and these children were three to four times more likely to be overweight.

Pausch suggested keeping a written record of your time spent watching television. Seeing this figure in black and white might convince you to cut back. If you tend to lose track of time while on the computer or watching television, you might want to set an egg timer for a particular amount of minutes. When it rings, your time in front of the screen is over.

You might wonder what you could do with all the extra time you'll find when you stop watching television or sitting in front of the computer. You could draw on your creative nature. Build a tree house, paint a mural on your bedroom wall, or write a novel. You might spend time with family and friends and do something fun. Go bowling, roller-skating, or out to a restaurant. You could even begin a charity club and perform a different community outreach project each month. The possibilities are unlimited.

Uncluttering your entire room is another responsible thing to do. You are being responsible to your parents by keeping your area of the home straightened. You are also taking responsibility for items you own. It might even keep you from being distracted from your studies. "Visual clutter interferes with smooth thinking," says Kutner.

You might want to ask a friend to help you sort through your things, so he or she can share honest input. Your friend will tell you to junk that old shirt that you're convinced you'll wear again one day even though it's out of style.

Here is a simple method to unclutter: In one pile, place the items you love and with which you refuse to part. Remember how much they mean to you and take good care of them. Throw out or recycle damaged and unusable items. In another pile, put the clothes you have that are still in good condition but that you have outgrown or haven't worn in one year. Also put items you no longer use or want in this pile. Give these things to the needy. "Share your abundance with the less fortunate," says Kutner. In this way, you have the added benefit of taking responsibility for other people.

BEING RESPONSIBLE AT WORK AND WITH MONEY

4

Work is love made visible.

—Kahlil Gibran (1883–1931),
Lebanese artist, writer, and philosopher

Part of being a responsible person is getting a job—even just a part-time job—and holding onto it. The first step is deciding what job is the best fit for you. In their book, *What Color is Your Parachute? for Teens,* authors Richard Nelson Bolles, Carol Christen, and Jean M. Blomquist say considering what you like to do and what you do best can lead you to a good job choice. Think about which school subjects are your favorites and at which you excel. Also, consider what you enjoy doing in your spare time. If you love environmental science and spend your free time hiking, a job as a nature guide at the state park might be perfect for you.

Take note of what your friends and teachers recognize as your strengths, suggests Lara Kaye Cifone, youth services coordinator for the nonprofit organization Hands On! The Hudson Valley, located in Poughkeepsie, New York. This will give you insight into talents you might not have realized you have. It may also point you toward a particular job. Cifone suggests that teens consider whether they want to start

A FIERY PASSION

From the time he was a child, Richard Muellerleile's bedroom was filled with fire trucks. Instead of reading comic books like other kids his age, he read magazines and biographies about firefighters and their adventures. At just 16 years old, Muellerleile decided to follow his passion and join the local fire corps as a volunteer junior firefighter. He began by doing basic jobs at the fires, such as rolling hoses and bringing firefighters the tools they needed. He was allowed to fight fires only from the outside of the structures. After much training, he was able to join the firefighters and bring interior fires under control.

Muellerleile explored another field for a little while when he was older and earned a two-year college degree in music education. Still, the pull to be a firefighter was strong. He knew he enjoyed medical courses, so he decided to study for two years to become a paramedic. Muellerleile did well in these classes.

Muellerleile interviewed for a job as a paramedic and firefighter for the Arlington Fire District in Poughkeepsie, New York. Naturally, the interviewer was pleased that Muellerleile had excelled at his paramedic training, on the firefighter's written exam, and on the physical ability test. In addition, his volunteer work weighed heavily in his favor. "One of the reasons they preferred me was my volunteer experience," Muellerleile explains. The interviewer was also impressed with the passion Muellerleile showed for the work. He was chosen for his dream job.

Muellerleile finds his job rewarding. He enjoys being the one who helps people through the "worst day of their lives." "I wouldn't trade my job for anything," he says, "not even to be a multibillionaire."

their own business, such as babysitting or tutoring, or if they wish to work for a company. Volunteering or interning also can help teens discover what they do well and enjoy doing. Although this kind of work doesn't typically earn money, volunteers and interns gain work experience and new skills.

Once a teen has decided on the type of employment he or she wants, Cifone suggests that networking is an effective way to actually find and land a part-time or summer job. *Networking* means building relationships with people who might help you in a specific field or job. Tell neighbors, your friends' parents, teachers, guidance counselors, and members of your community that you are seeking a particular type of work. They can suggest job possibilities for you. In addition, Cifone said that employers are more likely to hire a person who has been recommended to them by someone they trust.

Most teens applying for jobs will only need to fill out an application rather than present a résumé. However, if a résumé is requested, Cifone said to be sure to include volunteer work that has taught you work skills and demonstrates that you are a well-rounded individual. In addition, list your sports or after-school activities because they show dedication. Also, don't forget to mention academic honors. Employers understand that academic excellence often translates to excellence in the workplace. Finally, Cifone said employers like to see words and phrases such as *enthusiastic* and *willing to learn* on a young person's résumé.

If you are asked to interview for a job, Cifone said to be sure to do a bit of Internet research about the company before you go, so you can be an informed interviewee. Dress neatly and look professional for the interview. You should make eye contact with the interviewer, choose your words carefully, and answer questions honestly. The authors of *What Color is Your Parachute?* suggest sending a note to the interviewer afterward to thank him or her for taking the time to consider you for the position. This is not only polite, but will also help the interviewer remember you in a positive light.

Once you've landed your dream job, you must prove to be a responsible employee. Cifone noted that a responsible employee goes to work when scheduled and arrives on time. He or she treats the manager, coworkers, and customers with respect and patience. A responsible employee also shares enthusiasm and new ideas. "Bring creative and innovative thinking to the job," said Cifone. "Think outside the box." And don't hesitate to ask questions, which is the best way to learn to do things correctly.

MONEY MATTERS

Whether they earn a paycheck or an allowance, or are given birthday checks from relatives, many teens have money for which they are responsible. Jeffrey Wenzel, a financial advisor with Ameriprise Financial, said that being responsible with money begins with creating a budget. The budget lists any money you make, your income, and all fixed expenses. Expenses for an older teen might include car payments, auto insurance, gasoline, monthly cell phone bills, clothes, and concerts/movies. Many people also write a contribution to charity into their budgets. "Don't spend more than you make," said Wenzel.

Wenzel also advised, "No matter what, pay yourself first." This means taking a certain amount of your income and placing it in a savings account, where it will work for you by earning interest. Interest is an amount of money that a bank pays its customers for putting their funds there. Saving money is the way to build wealth.

In their book, *The ABCs of Making Money 4 Teens*, Dr. Denis Cauvier and Alan Lysaght say that you shouldn't confuse income with wealth. Income is what you make; wealth is how much you keep. Wealth offers you freedom and the opportunity to pursue many life goals. They say, "Remember, the acquisition of wealth isn't a goal, it's a tool to a wide variety of goals." Wenzel suggests setting long term goals for the money you save, such as saving for college and buying a car when you are old enough. Unless you are

CHILD LABOR

In the Industrial Revolution of the mid-1800s, the United States saw a sharp increase in child labor. Child laborers were children under 15 years of age who worked full-time. Factory and mine owners used children as inexpensive sources of labor. The children's families were extremely poor and relied on their children's wages to earn enough money to pay for necessities, such as food.

These children worked long hours—10 to 12 hours a day or longer—for little pay. They often worked in extremely hot or cold temperatures and in dangerous conditions. There was no time to attend school or play outside. Some children worked in the textile mills. Girls used their tiny hands to thread fibers through the machines. Boys climbed atop machines to replace bobbins—the spools that hold the thread for weaving—when they were empty. Other children worked in glass factories, where the temperatures could rise above 100°F (37°C). Boys in coal mining areas were hired as "breaker boys." They leaned over coal chutes and removed stones and slate from the coal supply. The breaker boys often had misshapen spines because of the many hours they spent bent over at work. Boys as young as 12 years old were paid to travel deep into the mine to retrieve coal.

A 1906 advertisement sponsored by the National Child Labor Committee depicts a young girl named Ola before and after her difficult job in a cotton mill and lets readers know about the issue of child labor. The ad was a call to action for people to join the committee and take a stand against child labor.

(continues)

(continued)

In many cities, poor immigrant families took on sewing jobs to be completed in the basement of their buildings or in their apartments. For example, the family might assemble men's suits or women's dresses. The children would hand-sew linings or attach buttons alongside their parents. Each family member would work late into the night.

People became outraged about child labor practices. In 1904, the National Child Labor Committee was formed by a group of people who fought for change in the country's laws. The Keating-Owens Act, passed in 1916, said that goods made by child laborers could not be shipped across state lines. However, only two years later, the U.S. Supreme Court judged the law unconstitutional and overturned it. Finally, in 1938, Congress passed the Fair Labor Standards Act, which required children to be 16 years old before working full-time.

Today, teenagers can read the updated Fair Labor Standards Act to discover regulations that govern their employment. The document discusses fair wages and acceptable work hours. It also lists jobs that are prohibited to those who are under 18 years of age, such as mining, roofing, and working with explosives.

taking money out of your savings to meet your long-term goals, Wenzel says savings should not be touched. "Think of savings as putting away for a rainy day, but only for a true downpour," he said.

Another strategy for building wealth is to be self-disciplined in your spending. Wenzel said people should not be swayed by society's obsession with spending money. You could keep a notebook and enter your daily purchases into it. Upon review, you might spot unnecessary buying or ways that you could reduce spending. For example, you could borrow books from the library rather than buy them, and you could take your lunch to school instead of purchasing food. Then you'll have more money to place in savings.

THE ORACLE OF OMAHA

Warren Buffett is a good example of someone who managed money well and used his passion and talent to build a successful career. Buffett was born in Omaha, Nebraska, on August 30, 1930, and was a child during the Great Depression

INVESTING MONEY

There's no point in saving your money at home when you could put it in the bank to earn interest. One thing to keep in mind is that, typically, the higher the interest offered, the higher the risk. A bank or credit union savings account, certificate of deposit, and federal government bonds guarantee your money, but the interest rates are usually low. Higher interest rates can be earned in mutual fund or index fund investments, but your money is not guaranteed. In other words, the possibility exists that you could lose your money.

Mutual funds are pools of stocks and bonds managed by a professional known as a mutual fund manager. This manager decides which stocks and bonds to buy and sell, and you pay fees for this service. If you decide to invest in mutual funds, look for no-load funds, which are funds without a sales fee. Index funds are funds in which stocks and bonds are bought to mirror those found in a particular market index, such as the S&P 500. Because index funds don't require the active management that mutual funds do, the fees are usually lower. Before investing, it is vital that you thoroughly research your choices. You might even decide to visit a professional financial advisor for help with your investment decisions.

Think of investing this way: Let's say that at 15 years old, you start investing $100 each month in a savings opportunity that earns 8 percent interest annually. Each year the savings opportunity pays you $8 in interest for every $100 you have invested. By the time you reach 55, you would have put $48,000 of your money into savings, but because of the added interest, the total in the account would be nearly $350,000.

(1929 to around 1938). The poverty of this period most likely influenced his interest in making money. He was driven to earn money and had a knack for doing so. In addition, Buffett was talented at math and fascinated with the stock market and how companies did business.

Buffett was always on the lookout for ways to earn money. Like many children, Buffett had a lemonade stand; however, he made sure that his lemonade stand was on the busiest street in the area, so he could make the most profit. He searched for lost golf balls at a local golf course and sold them. When he lived near Washington, D.C., Buffett worked diligently on five newspaper routes and delivered nearly 500 papers daily. He made $175 a month. When he was just 15 years old, he and his friend Donald Danly began a business by fixing a pinball machine and putting it in the local barbershop. Soon, they had a few machines in various locations around town.

Young Buffett wasn't only working to make money. He was also trying his hand at investment. When he was 11 years old, he bought stock in Cities Service Preferred for $38 per share. He sold the stock when it was worth $40 per share, which meant that he made $2 in profit on each share. Soon after, however, the stock rose to $200 per share. That experience taught Buffett to be patient. At only 14 years old, Buffett had already saved $1,200, which he used to invest in 40 acres of farmland in Nebraska.

Buffett attended college at the Wharton School at the University of Pennsylvania for two years and completed his college studies at the University of Nebraska at Lincoln. He earned his graduate degree from Columbia University, where he learned many valuable lessons about investing. He found the investing philosophy of his professor, Benjamin Graham, to be especially insightful.

Buffett made most of his money through smart investing. He believed in studying everything about a business and its potential before investing in it. Over the years, Buffet has

Warren Buffet found major success through studying business, working hard, and smart investing, but he did not forget about his social responsibilities. His donation to the Bill and Melinda Gates Foundation is the largest charitable gift ever made. Here he stands in 2006 with a stock certificate representing 121,737 Class B shares of BerkshireHathaway Inc., the company of which he is the largest shareholder and CEO.

bought shares in many companies, such as Geico and Coca-Cola. Currently, Buffett is the chairman, CEO, and major stockholder of the company Berkshire Hathaway. In 2008, *Forbes* magazine named him the richest man in the world, with a worth of $62 billion.

Through it all, Buffett has been careful not to overspend. He has a yearly salary of $100,000—much less than many top business people—and leaves the rest invested in his company. He drives his own reasonably priced car, and he still lives in the same cozy Omaha home that he bought in 1958.

Throughout his career, Buffett was often criticized for not giving more of his money to charity. He knew he was talented at investing money and felt that it would be better if he continued to make money during his lifetime and then leave the money to charitable organizations upon his death. In 2006, he changed his mind and donated 85 percent of his wealth to charity. The majority of the donation went to the Bill and Melinda Gates Foundation, which is an organization that focuses on improving education and health among people throughout the world. The gift consisted of Berkshire Hathaway B shares, which in 2006 were estimated to be worth $37 billion. Since the donation was in shares and not cash, the amount of the donation increases as the value of the shares increase in the stock market. Buffett's donation is the largest charitable gift ever made.

FREEGANS: REJECTING CONSUMERISM

People can also learn lessons from freegans about being responsible stewards of money and of the environment, although their practices might be too extreme for some. *Freegan* is a combination of the words *free* and *vegan*. Participants in the freegan lifestyle don't consume any animal products or use anything tested on animals. They reject the consumerism and waste that they observe in U.S. culture. They believe that manufacturing processes contribute to many societal ills, such as pollution, sweatshop labor, and

Freegans take responsibility for money and the environment in a manner that may be a bit extreme for some people. Eating dicarded food is among the many things they do to practice rejection of consumer waste. Here, freegans (*left to right*) Madeline Nelson, Kirsten Stade, Kabi Jorgensen, and Janet Kalish forage through garbage bags in front of a supermarket in New York City in 2005.

global warming, so they do not purchase anything unless it is absolutely necessary.

Instead of buying things, freegans participate in "urban foraging," also known as "dumpster diving." They search through garbage to find useable food or a variety of products, from books to bicycles. They offer found items that they don't need free of charge through networks such as the Web site www.freecycle.org.

Freegans compost, recycle, and reuse to reduce waste. They don't use disposable items. Instead, for example, they will use mugs instead of plastic cups or rags rather than paper towels. If something must be purchased, freegans buy secondhand.

In addition, freegans don't want to depend on fossil fuels. They use alternative methods of transportation, such as walking or bicycling. If a car is necessary, they try to convert diesel engines to engines that run on fryer oil discarded from restaurants.

Another strategy freegans use is wild foraging. They search for fresh food and medicinal plants in the woods or city parks. Often, they take unused lots of land, turn them into community gardens, and grow their own produce.

Freegans are often able to leave their jobs because they have less need of money. They spend the extra time with family, volunteering, or working as activists for social causes. One warning about the freegan lifestyle: Be aware that some of the strategies they encourage are illegal. For example, they believe in hopping trains without buying a ticket as an alternative form of transportation, and in "squatting," living free in abandoned buildings, instead of paying for a home.

BEING RESPONSIBLE ON THE INTERNET

When I took office only high energy physicists had ever heard of what is called the Worldwide Web . . . Now even my cat has its own page.

—U.S. President Bill Clinton (1946–   )

The computer and Internet are amazing innovations. They can make your life easier and allow you to expand your knowledge and friendships. You can visit fascinating Web sites, such as NASA's site, where you can see pictures of a crater on Mars that looks like a happy face. You can e-mail friends with the latest news. However, you need to use the Internet responsibly to make all your high-tech experiences positive ones.

In security expert Gavin de Becker's book, *Protecting the Gift*, he says to remember that nothing written on the Internet is truly private. "Don't include anything in a Web site that you would not be willing to post on the bulletin board of every supermarket in every city in America," he says. This advice is important to keep in mind, especially if you are e-mailing or posting on a social networking site.

You can be responsible in your use of e-mail. Be careful not to reveal personal information through your choice of e-mail address, warns Mark Hoops, the senior consumer frauds representative for the New York State Attorney General's office. To safeguard against identity theft, don't use your name or home address as part of your e-mail address. Also, as further protection from child predators, young people should choose an e-mail address that does not reveal their gender (for example, no addresses like "qtgirl").

Beware of e-mail scam artists, who use e-mail to steal your private information. These e-mails are fashioned to look as if they were sent from your financial institution or a well-known company. However, if you click on the link in the e-mail, you may be sent to the scammer's Web site. There, if you provide any personal information, such as your Social Security number or bank account, your identity could be stolen. Other e-mail scams say that you can share in lottery winnings, but the con men only want to steal your money. "Don't believe scams about getting things free or fast money," says school psychologist Jennifer Obrizok. In addition, be cautious when opening e-mail attachments, which can contain viruses that will affect your hard drive. Have an antivirus program installed on your computer for protection.

You should also be careful when e-mailing people you know. While communicating via e-mail, think about how your words will be interpreted by the receiver. Remember that the person receiving your note can't see the expression on your face or hear the tone of your voice, which leaves plenty of room for misunderstandings. You might mean something as a joke, but your friend might take your comment seriously. In addition, don't contribute to spam by forwarding chain letters that promise good fortune or threaten bad luck. At best, they are bothersome. At worst, they can upset a person.

Obrizok warns of the "faceless" nature of the Internet. "You can't see to whom you are talking on the Internet, so you can't take what they say as truth," she says. Child

THE CONSEQUENCES OF CYBERBULLYING

A responsible person needs to consider the consequences of his or her actions on the Internet. Cyberbullying is not only cruel behavior, but it can also have devastating results, as in the case of Megan Meier.

Megan was a 13-year-old girl from Dardenne Prairie, Missouri. She had a difficult childhood because she was bullied at school and suffered from attention deficit disorder and depression. Her parents allowed her to set up a MySpace page to communicate with friends. One day, a 16-year-old boy named Josh Evans, whom Megan thought was cute, started contacting her on MySpace.

In an effort to put an end to online bullying, Tina Meier testifies before the Internet Harassment Task Force in 2007 about the weakness in Missouri's laws. Her 13-year-old daughter, Megan, committed suicide in 2006 after being hurt by vicious online bullying.

He said he was new to the area and was homeschooled. They e-mailed back and forth for more than a month, and Megan believed they had formed a friendship. Josh sent complimentary e-mails to Megan, who had low self-esteem and loved to read his positive comments.

Suddenly, on October 15, 2006, Josh's communications became insulting. He wrote, "I don't know if I want to be friends with you any

(continues)

(continued)

longer because I hear you are not nice to your friends." The next day, he sent cruel e-mails to Megan and posted negative statements about her on electronic bulletin boards. His last e-mail said, "The world would be a better place without you." Megan's mother, Tina, became upset with her when she saw the objectionable language Megan was using online, and they had an argument. Megan raced up to her room, and 20 minutes later, Megan's mother discovered that Megan had hanged herself in her closet. She was pronounced dead the next day.

Six weeks following Megan's death, it was discovered that Josh Evans did not exist. Lori Drew, the mother of one of Megan's former friends, and Drew's 18-year-old assistant had allegedly set up a fake MySpace page and created the fictional Josh Evans. Drew said she only wanted to find out what Megan was saying about her daughter. On November 26, 2008, Drew was found guilty of accessing protected computers without authorization, although the other woman involved has admitted to sending many of the cruel e-mails. Almost eight months later, U.S. District Judge George Wu tentatively threw out Drew's conviction. This is a complicated case that will probably be in the courts for a long time.

Tina Meier has founded the Megan Meier Foundation in her daughter's memory. The foundation seeks to prevent bullying and cyberbullying by encouraging laws that make cyberbullying illegal. The foundation also educates parents and students about these cruel practices. Megan's mother doesn't want any other family to suffer the loss that her family has faced.

predators sometimes pose as children or teens with the intent of hurting those with whom they communicate. Don't share personal information with someone online and never agree to meet anyone you befriend on the Internet in person.

If you have a Web page on a social networking site, such as MySpace or Facebook, or if you submit videos to You-Tube, be careful to protect your identifying information. For example, don't wear a school T-shirt in your photographs. In addition, don't post photographs or write anything that might harm your reputation. "You have to think about who might see it," says Hoops. School administrators, potential employers, and police officers looking for illegal behavior may view your Web page or video submission. Consider also that items on the Internet float around for a long time. Before posting anything, "Ask yourself, 'Would I want my grandchildren to see this?'" Obrizok said.

Another danger of the faceless Internet is cyberbullying. This is cruelty to others that takes place online. Hoops said that cyberbullying occurs because people find it easier to say mean or threatening things on the Internet, things they wouldn't dare say in person. A responsible person is respectful even if he or she isn't face to face with the other individual. "Treat others the way you would want to be treated," Obrizok says.

SMART SURFING

Whether you are surfing the Web for pleasure or to complete a research paper, it's best to visit sites with good reputations. In *Cyber-Safe Kids, Cyber-Savvy Teens*, author Nancy E. Willard says it is important to know what organization has created a particular site. For example, the well-respected Mayo Clinic in Minnesota founded a site (www.mayoclinic.com), so people can feel confident visiting it to find health information. To determine what kind of organization is behind a Web site, it is helpful to learn to decipher a uniform resource locator (URL). Site addresses that end in *.edu* are academic institution sites, *.gov* are government sites, *.mil* are military sites, *.com* are generally commercial sites, and *.org* are usually private or nonprofit sites.

The Internet has many positive Web sites to visit that can inspire responsible behavior. Discover the stories of real-life heroes at www.giraffe.org. This Web site is home to the nonprofit The Giraffe Heroes Project, which tells the stories of heroes who "stick their necks out for the common good." Here you can read about people like Michael Munds, a young boy who suffers from Treacher-Collins syndrome, which causes skull and facial malformations. When Michael heard about the April 9, 1995 bombing of the Alfred P. Murrah Federal Building in Oklahoma City, he organized a bowl-a-thon that raised $37,649 to help the victims. It was the most money donated to the cause by anyone in the United States.

On the Giraffe Heroes Web site, you can also learn about Mimi Silbert, who founded Delancey Street, which as of 2008 had five locations across the United States. This is a two-year program that helps ex-convicts, recovering drug addicts, and homeless individuals learn job skills and earn at least a high school equivalency diploma. To date, Delancey Street has helped 14,000 people to become productive members of society.

Another inspiring Web site is myhero.com, sponsored by the nonprofit My Hero Project. On this site you can browse stories about heroes from all walks of life, from teaching to science. For example, one of the articles highlights Chief Wilma Mankiller, who was the first female principal chief of the Cherokee Nation. Another tells about the life of Dian Fossey and her study of mountain gorillas in Zaire (now the Democratic Republic of the Congo) and Rwanda. Fossey's stand against gorilla poachers led to the protection of the gorillas by the Rwandan government.

You can visit Web sites that help you connect to volunteer opportunities and offer ideas for charitable outreach. Do Something (www.dosomething.org) is an organization that challenges visitors to chose a charitable cause and support it. It lists projects in which people can become involved and highlights celebrities and their outreach choices. Surf to www.idealist.org, supported by the nonprofit organization Action Without Borders, where you can investigate volunteer opportunities and chances to participate in internships. At the Ziv Tzedakah Fund Web site (www.ziv.org) you can click

Wilma Mankiller, seen here in 2005, became the first female principal chief of the Cherokee Nation. Her strength and determination helped her change the way her people viewed women and their roles in leadership positions.

LAWBREAKERS PROVIDE OWN EVIDENCE

On March 30, 2008, eight teenagers from Lakeland, Florida, were charged with brutally beating a 16-year-old girl and videotaping the attack with the intent of posting it on YouTube. Six girls participated in the beating, while two boys acted as lookouts. The victim was so severely hurt that her vision and hearing were affected, not to mention the lasting psychological damage she suffered. The beating was a twisted attempt to gain Internet celebrity. Now, the tape will be used as evidence in the trials against the participants.

on "Useful Articles" and find Danny Siegel's 116 practical ideas for charitable projects. It suggests, for example, going to the area dry cleaners and offering to distribute unclaimed items to the needy. Another suggestion is to buy extra food during each trip to the grocery store to give to the hungry.

Cyber-Safe Kids, Cyber-Savvy Teens also discusses some of the negative Web sites that exist. These Web sites are created by harmful groups and should be avoided. Some Web sites spread hatred against others based upon race, ethnicity, religion, or sexual orientation. Other Web sites preach violence toward schoolmates. There are also pro-anorexia and pro-bulimia Web sites that encourage behaviors associated with life-threatening eating disorders. In most cases, emotionally troubled individuals are behind these kinds of Web sites.

ILLEGAL INTERNET ACTIVITIES

Acting responsibly on the Web also includes giving others the proper credit for their ideas and creations. While doing Internet research for school papers, be certain not to copy and paste the ideas of others and represent them as your own. This is plagiarism, and it is unethical because it is stealing another's intellectual work. It is also illegal—you can be sued by the original author. Simply use quotation marks or para-phrase small bits of text (generally up to three sentences is okay, as long as you attribute the text to the true author) and always credit your source. Illegally downloading music and movies is also stealing because the artists are not receiving pay for their work.

6 RESPONSIBILITY FOR OTHERS

For unto whomsoever much is given, of him shall be much required.

—The Bible, *Luke 12:48*

You are responsible for your own day-to-day obligations and life's goals. You can also consider being responsible for other people. Charitable outreach improves the lives of those you help and, in turn, enriches the community. You can appreciate the benefits of charitable work in the following story of Louis J. Acompora and Kaitlin Forbes.

Louis J. Acompora was a talented 14-year-old lacrosse player. He was the captain and goalie of his freshman high school team in Northport, New York. On March 25, 2000, during his first game, Louis blocked a shot with his chest, and he dropped to the ground. The blow to his chest affected his heart at the exact moment it was recharging, and his heart went into ventricular fibrillation. In ventricular fibrillation, the heart quivers like Jell-O, and it can't pump blood through the body. Tragically, Louis's heart—and then his breathing—stopped, and he died of sudden cardiac arrest.

Despite their grief, Louis's parents, John and Karen, began the Louis J. Acompora Foundation. They realized that Louis might have lived if a machine called an automated external defibrillator (AED) had been at the school. The AED could have shocked Louis's heart back to its normal rhythm. The Acomporas fought to pass a law requiring every New York State school to have an AED. They didn't want anyone else to face the loss that they had suffered. The law, known as Louis's Law, was passed on May 7, 2002.

Fast-forward three years: Like Louis, 15-year-old Kaitlin Forbes was a dedicated athlete. She played on her high school varsity volleyball, basketball, and softball teams in Rhinebeck, New York. On May 11, 2005, Kaitlin was racing to first base on her high school softball field. She looked at the first baseman and said, "I don't feel well." She collapsed. Her heart wasn't beating, and she wasn't breathing.

Kaitlin's physical education teacher realized that she had suffered sudden cardiac arrest. He had one student call 911, another fetch the nurse, and a third bring the school's AED. He began cardio-pulmonary resuscitation (CPR) to keep Kaitlin's blood and oxygen flowing to her brain. Then, the AED was used to shock Kaitlin's heart back to a regular rhythm. Kaitlin's life was saved by both the well-trained human heroes that day, and by the AED placed at the school thanks to the Acomporas and Louis's Law.

Just 14 months later, Kaitlin's close friend and teammate, 17-year-old Maggie O'Malley, died at home of sudden cardiac arrest. Both Maggie and Kaitlin had undiagnosed myocarditis, an abnormal swelling of the heart, which contributed to their sudden cardiac arrests. Kaitlin was determined to help prevent sudden cardiac deaths in the future. With the help of Kaitlin's mother, Linda, and Maggie's mother, Pat, Kaitlin founded the Heart Safe Club.

The members of the Heart Safe Club—most of whom are teenagers—are certified in CPR and AED use and are CPR and AED instructors. The members teach frequent CPR classes to community members and school students. They organize community heart screenings, so any heart problems can be detected early. In addition, the club persuaded the town of Rhinebeck, New York, to place AEDs in all of its public buildings, such as the town hall and village garage. Kaitlin also has been a vocal supporter of a law that will require all New York State high schools to certify students in CPR and AED use before they graduate. She knows firsthand the value of this lifesaving training. The motto of the Heart Safe Club is "Heroes aren't born. They are trained."

Kaitlin's outreach to others doesn't end with her volunteer activities. She plans to attend medical school and specialize in cardiology. Her story is a wonderful example of people taking responsibility for one another. The Acomporas' caring as well as the knowledgeable heroes on the scene were responsible for saving Kaitlin's life. And Kaitlin is passing their lifesaving gift forward to others.

IT FEELS GOOD TO DO GOOD

There are many reasons why you should reach out to other people. Consider how helping people can make their lives easier and happier. In turn, you will feel good, too. "There is nothing that will give you a greater sense of self-worth than making a difference in someone else's life," says Nancy Kelly, a clinical social worker. "Charitable outreach gives you a sense of connection, belonging, and accomplishment."

Allan Luks is a lawyer and the former executive director of the New York City branch of Big Brothers Big Sisters—a national mentoring program. In Luks's book, *The Healing Power of Doing Good*, he discusses his study of 3,296 people that demonstrated how helping others literally made the participants feel good. Of the volunteers in the study who filled out a questionnaire, 95 percent reported experiencing a "helper's high" when they performed charitable acts. It was a feeling similar to the one runners experience with the release of endorphins, chemicals in the brain that are linked to feelings of happiness. In addition, the study participants benefited from long-lasting feelings of well-being: 57 percent reported an increased feeling of self-worth, and 53 percent said they felt happier and more optimistic and experienced a decrease in feelings of help-lessness and depression.

Charitable giving also has an effect on the brain that can be measured. Researchers Jordan Grafman and Jorge Moll conducted a fascinating study of altruism at the National Institutes of Health. Daniel Stimson reported their find-ings on the National Institute of Neurological Disorders and Stroke Web site. The researchers instructed 20 subjects to play a computer game in which they could win money to give to charity. While they were playing, the experimenters performed brain scans on the subjects. When a participant chose to give money away, the midbrain—the portion deep in the brain that responds to pleasure—lit up. The experiment showed that there is actual physical pleasure in giving.

Charitable outreach has another added side benefit: It can increase your skills. For example, depending on what kind of charity you decide to start or help, you could learn anything from training dogs to building houses.

FIRST STEPS TO CHARITY

You can decide which charitable cause is right for you by choosing something about which you feel passionate. If you can't pass a puppy without petting it, a charity that addresses animals' needs might be for you. Also, consider your talents. If you and your friends are excellent Irish step dancers and you love little kids, maybe you could teach a dance class at the local after-school program.

Of course, making a large charitable commitment might seem overwhelming in addition to your studies, sports, and other extracurricular activities. Yet, outreach can be done in small ways in your everyday life, and you could start with your family. For example, imagine that your younger sister has been bugging your mom to teach her to ride a bicycle without training wheels. You can offer to run her up and down the driveway until she can manage to do it solo. With just a little time and effort, you would have started your sister on an activity that could keep her healthy for the rest of her life. She might even become the next Lance Armstrong.

Keep your eyes open for opportunities to share acts of kindness in your neighborhood, as well. Allowing a young mother with two crying children to cut in front of you in a grocery store line would be greatly appreciated. Perhaps you could take the garbage can to the curb or shovel a snowy driveway for an elderly neighbor. At school, a genuine smile or a heartfelt compliment can turn around a classmate's day. If you are especially talented in one subject area, maybe you could be a peer tutor.

EVERYDAY CHARITY

Jason Heigl is one person who made a big difference with small acts of kindness. Heigl was the older brother of actress Katherine Heigl. However, Jason was a star in his own right. In her book *Teach Your Kids to Care*, author Deborah Spaide wrote about how Jason fought against injustices he encountered in his everyday life. In high school, Jason was one of the popular students. One day, he saw a group of teenagers calling a girl named Linda "Fatso." He became angry. The very next day, he met Linda and walked her to her class. They became good friends. Soon, many of Jason's other friends got to know Linda and befriended her, as well. His act of kindness brightened Linda's entire high school experience.

In the fall of 1986, when Jason was only 15 years old, he was involved in a car accident in New Canaan, Connecticut. He was in the back of a pickup truck when it crashed. He was thrown from the truck and suffered massive head injuries. Tragically, he was declared brain dead. His family made the difficult decision to donate Jason's organs. His heart, kidneys, and corneas were transplanted, which gave others a chance to have healthy lives. Jason's sister, Katherine, and his mother, Nancy Heigl, have become public advocates for organ donation. "I always felt that Jason's organs were his last gift to the world for which he had great affection," Nancy said.

Actress Katherine Heigl (*left*) and her mother, Nancy (*right*), are public advocates for organ donation and were honored by the National Coalition on Donation in 2005. Their family donated son Jason's organs to patients in need after he was declared brain dead in 1986.

When you are ready to consider expanding your volunteer activities, it isn't difficult to find a worthy nonprofit organization to support. You might visit your local library and do a bit of research, or perform an Internet search. For example, type "environmental charities" into a search engine. Then, visit any organization's Web site that interests you and see if its goals fit well with yours.

In her book, *A Kid's Guide to Giving*, author Freddi Zeiler suggests visiting a Web site that evaluates charities before making a final decision about which charity to support. One such Web site is www.charitynavigator.org. This particular site rates charities according to how effectively they use contributions to meet their goals. Charities with four stars are considered the best. If you are going to give your money or time, you should be certain of the organization's qualifications.

THE MANY KINDS OF NONPROFIT ORGANIZATIONS

It might be simpler to choose which nonprofit you would like to help if you think about general categories of charitable organizations that address the following: poverty, animals, health, environmental concerns, human rights, the disabled, and the community.

To fight poverty, you could make hero sandwiches for the local soup kitchen. Or, you might lend your support to a national organization, such as America's Second Harvest, which has food banks across the United States that supply food to the hungry. Do you worry about people asleep on park benches in frigid weather? Reach out to your local homeless shelter by collecting and donating blankets or toiletries.

John Cahill, a 16-year-old from Salt Point, New York, decided to dedicate two weeks of his summer to help the poor. He joined a group of his friends and traveled with the Appalachia Service Project to West Virginia. There, he lent a hand building wheelchair ramps and insulating basements for people who needed these things but had no money to pay for them. When he returned home, Cahill said, "I will remember the looks on the peoples' faces when they saw the final project. The project is tangible, but the happiness you bring their hearts is intangible."

If you love animals, an animal-related nonprofit could be right for you. You could walk dogs at your local animal shelter. You might reach out to the American Society for the Prevention of Cruelty to Animals (ASPCA), which has a long tradition of saving pets from abusive situations and finding loving families to adopt them. On the other hand, if you feel the call of the wild, you may want to work with the World Wildlife Fund, which works to protect endangered species, such as the giant panda.

Perhaps you've had a loved one who has been stricken with a disease, such as cystic fibrosis or cancer, or you have been diagnosed with an illness. Then you may be especially motivated to support a health-related organization that is researching a cure for the disease or offers comfort to sufferers of that disease. Two examples of this kind of nonprofit are St. Jude Children's Research Hospital, which both provides care to seriously ill children and tries to find cures for their diseases, and the Cystic Fibrosis Foundation, which has the goal of finding a cure for cystic fibrosis.

Environmental organizations might interest you if you are diligent about recycling newspapers and cans or you only buy wood products that are Forest Stewardship Council certified. You might investigate organizations such as Ryan's Well Foundation, begun by Ryan Hreljac. Ryan became interested in building clean water sources in Africa when he was just 6 years old. In school, he had learned that people in Africa were dying because they didn't have clean water to drink. In 1999, Ryan raised $70 and purchased his first well in a Ugandan village. To date, Ryan's Well Foundation has raised millions of dollars and provided 329 wells in 14 countries.

You could investigate human rights organizations if you want to do something about children who labor endless hours in sweatshops making clothes. Human rights nonprofits address many different problems affecting people all over the world, from the education of women in countries where they are considered second-class citizens to freeing political prisoners.

BUILDING A BETTER WORLD

During his term as the 39th president of the United States, Jimmy Carter devoted much of his attention to furthering international peace. He helped to negotiate the Camp David Accords, which led to the signing of a 1979 peace treaty between Egypt and Israel. On June 18, 1979, President Carter signed the Strategic Arms Limitation Talks (SALT II) treaty with the Soviet Union. The treaty limited the amount of nuclear weapons that each country could produce.

President Carter's outreach did not end with his time in the White House. In 1982, he founded The Carter Center with the goal of furthering human rights and putting a halt to unnecessary human suffering. One of the center's major accomplishments is helping to nearly eliminate Guinea worm disease around the world. Guinea worm disease is caused by a parasite and causes painful symptoms in human beings. The incidence of Guinea worm disease has been reduced by 99.5 percent in Africa and Asia.

President Carter and his wife, Rosalynn, are active participants with Habitat for Humanity. Habitat for Humanity helps to build homes for those in need. The family for whom the house is being constructed works side by side with volunteers to build the home. When the house is complete, Habitat for Humanity sells the home to the family without making a profit and offers the family a no-interest loan. President Carter and his wife devote an entire week each year to Habitat for Humanity. During that week they can be found

You might choose to support an organization for the disabled. Perhaps you could become a puppy raiser for a guide dog foundation, such as Guiding Eyes for the Blind. A puppy raiser teaches a puppy basic obedience and helps it become used to humans, other pets, and new experiences so that the dog may one day guide a visually impaired individual. Or, you could volunteer for the Special Olympics, which offers

Former president Jimmy Carter and his wife, Rosalynn, volunteer for Habitat for Humanity every year. Here, they volunteer in Hungary in 1998 as part of the "Habitat for Humanity International" plan, which Jimmy Carter helped organize.

swinging hammers and putting up wallboard, along with thousands of other volunteers.

On December 10, 2002, President Carter was honored for all of his efforts when he was awarded the Nobel Peace Prize.

intellectually disabled people a chance to compete in athletic events.

Don't forget the community service organizations in your town or city. The local library could always use an expert book shelver or someone to teach computer classes for adults or craft classes to kids. You could even volunteer to help the fire department or ambulance corps.

SPECIFIC WAYS TO HELP

Once you've settled on the type of charitable organization you wish to support, how will you help? Charitable outreach can take many forms. You might decide to support an organization financially. You could set aside a certain percentage of your weekly allowance or paycheck to donate. Many churches request that their members give 10 percent of their income to the church, which is known as tithing. However, the amount you choose to give to a charitable organization is a personal matter and any amount would be appreciated.

You might participate in fundraisers and let others help you raise money. At Rutgers University in New Jersey, students hold an annual dance marathon to benefit the Embrace Kids Foundation for children with cancer and blood diseases. The Rutgers students commit to dancing for 32 hours and people pledge money to support the dancers. Between 1998 and 2008, participants raised more than $1.6 million for the nonprofit foundation.

Another way to raise funds is to sell items and give the proceeds to your favorite charity. Let's say you are good at making crafts. You could bead bracelets or fashion wooden carvings to sell. How about organizing a neighborhood carnival with games and contests? No one said raising money for charities shouldn't be fun!

Some charities welcome the donation of goods. Give old towels and blankets to an animal shelter. Those once-used galoshes or the bunny sweater Aunt Gertie gave you for your birthday could be given to the Salvation Army. If you check

THE IMPACT OF THE INDIVIDUAL

Kimmie Weeks was born in Liberia in Africa. When he was 9 years old, his country was involved in a bloody civil war. At that time, Weeks remembers being so hungry and thirsty that he was forced to eat roots and drink polluted water. He became terribly ill. The townsmen were certain that he would die, so they dug a grave for him. Miraculously, Weeks survived and has been making a difference in the lives of others ever since.

Kimmie Weeks's horrible experiences growing up in war-torn Liberia inspired him to devote his life to ending human suffering—a purpose he has actively worked toward since a young age.

Weeks's horrible experiences sparked his passion to ease the suffering of children in Africa. At only 13 years of age, he founded Voice of the Future to fight for children's rights in Liberia. At 15, he started the Children's Disarmament Campaign, which, together with the United Nations Children's Fund (UNICEF), helped disarm 20,000 child soldiers. The next year, he established the Children's Bureau of Information to help former child soldiers begin new, productive lives in society.

Weeks wrote and published a controversial report about the Liberian Army's training of child soldiers. His life was threatened, so he fled to the United States, where he was granted asylum—a safe place to live. In the United States, he began Youth Action International (www.youthactioninternational.org), which gives young people the opportunity to become involved in humanitarian activities in Africa. Among its many projects, the organization builds orphanages and schools, helps former child soldiers, and teaches job skills to women and children.

their Web sites, many organizations include wish lists of items that they need.

Finally, and probably most appreciated, is giving your time and talents in a hands-on way. If you know how to create artistic scrapbook pages, for example, you could visit a nursing home and teach the residents how it's done. Not only would you be passing on a welcomed skill, but you would also be sharing conversation with the elderly participants who might not have many visitors.

Volunteering time is linked to better health and longer life. The Corporation for National and Community Service reviewed existing research in its publication, *The Health Benefits of Volunteering.* "Volunteers have greater longevity, higher functional ability, lower rates of depression and less incidence of heart disease," the organization concluded.

Maybe you have a passion for a cause that isn't being addressed by anyone else. Start your own organization and you can make an impact, just like Kaitlin Forbes, Ryan Hreljac, and Kimmie Weeks did.

Debbe Magnusen is another person who founded her own organization. During the years before she started her non-profit, Magnusen and her family fostered 30 drug-exposed infants in their Costa Mesa, California, home. They even adopted five of the babies. Magnusen felt very sad when she heard about babies being abandoned in unsafe places. She decided to do something to help prevent infant abandonment: She started Project Cuddle.

In 1996, Magnusen published a crisis hotline telephone number for pregnant mothers to use if they needed help. The phone number rang right in the living room of Magnusen's house. She would connect these frightened women with whatever services they required. She might find them adoption lawyers or professionals who could help them keep their babies. As of 2008, more than 600 infants have been saved by Project Cuddle and Magnusen's devotion.

Consider being responsible for others in both small and larger ways. It will make the world a better place and be fulfilling to you, as well.

7

ALTRUISM: THE ULTIMATE IN RESPONSIBILITY

A man does what he must—in spite of personal consequences, in spite of obstacles and dangers and pressures—and that is the basis of all human morality.

—U.S. President John F. Kennedy (1917–1963)

Throughout history, there have been remarkable individuals who have displayed extraordinarily responsible behavior toward others. Their behavior can be considered altruistic, which means that it is marked by unselfish devotion to the welfare of others.

Samuel P. Oliner was just 12 years old during World War II when he and his family—his father, stepmother, two half-brothers, half-sister, and grandfather and his wife—were forced by the Nazis to live in the Jewish ghetto Bobowa in Poland. One day, Nazi soldiers came to take them away. Samuel's stepmother frantically instructed him to run and hide. He obeyed her and hid on a rooftop until all the residents and soldiers were gone.

Young Samuel then made the long journey to a Christian childhood schoolmate of his father's, Balwina Piecuch. On the way, he met a farmer who told him that the Jews from Bobowa had been taken to the woods and forced to undress, before they were shot and left in a mass grave. Samuel's entire family was dead.

When Samuel reached Piecuch, she risked her own safety by hiding him in her home. Over the next days, she gave him a Christian name and taught him Catholic prayers and principles. This way, he could escape detection by the Nazis if they questioned his religion. Samuel left Piecuch's home because the risk of discovery became too great. He found work as a farmhand, and Piecuch's son visited him every so often to warn him of Nazi danger in the area. Samuel survived.

Young Samuel Oliner's rescue by the very unselfish Piecuch during the war inspired an adult Oliner to study the altruism of non-Jewish rescuers of Jews during World War II. His study is the subject of the book, *The Altruistic Personality: Rescuers of Jews in Nazi Europe*, written by Oliner and his wife, Pearl. In it, the Oliners define altruism using the following criteria: "1. It is directed towards helping another. 2. It involves a high risk or sacrifice to the actor. 3. It is accomplished by no external rewards. 4. It is voluntary." They go even further to define "conventional altruism" as not life threatening to the helper, and "heroic altruism" as involving greater risk to the helper.

The Oliners' study involved detailed interviews with 700 people: 406 rescuers, 126 nonrescuers, and 150 survivors of the Holocaust. The Oliners wanted to discover why the rescuers risked their lives to save Jews. They wondered if altruism—this extraordinary sense of responsibility toward others—could be taught.

Through their interviews, the Oliners found that rescuers had parents who modeled and taught caring behavior toward others. The rescuers' parents expected their children to meet high standards when it came to acting generously toward others and not seeking anything in return. The rescuers also had a developed sense of empathy toward others, meaning they were sensitive to the feelings and experiences of other people.

In addition, the parents of rescuers taught their children that all people were equal, no matter their religion or economic status. Therefore, the rescuers were more likely to reach out to Jews because they viewed them in a positive light, as equals.

Interestingly, the Oliners discovered that rescuers came from homes in which parents disciplined them using reason. For example, if a child broke one of the parents' rules, they would talk to the child about the importance of being obedient instead of spanking him or her. Children who were treated with this type of respect were likely to be kind and generous people. On the other hand, nonrescuers were more likely to have received physical punishments handed out by frustrated or angry parents.

The following are stories of altruistic people who took responsibility toward others to the highest degree. They can inspire us to live our most responsible lives.

TO LAY DOWN ONE'S LIFE FOR A FRIEND

During World War II, four U.S. Army chaplains—Lt. Alexander Goode, a Jewish rabbi; Lt. John Washington, a Roman Catholic priest; Lt. Clark Poling, a Dutch Reformed minister; and Lt. George Fox, a Methodist minister—were traveling together aboard the U.S. Army transport ship USAT *Dorchester*. The ship was carrying 902 military men, merchant seamen, and civilian workers en route to the Army base in Greenland.

Many of the men became seasick on the voyage, and they were nervous about the war dangers that lay ahead. The four chaplains worked to raise their spirits. They prayed with the men, comforted them, and joked with them.

On February 2, 1943, the ship was making its way through the waters off the coast of Newfoundland. The *Tampa*, one

Former U.S. president Harry Truman looks up at a mural at the Four Chaplains Chapel in Philadelphia in 1951. The mural honors the four chaplains who heroically gave their lives to help others aboard the USAT *Dorchester* in 1943.

of the Coast Guard cutters accompanying the *Dorchester*, detected a German submarine in the area. The *Dorchester*'s captain told the men to sleep in their clothes and life jackets in case of an emergency. However, many of the men chose to sleep only in their underwear because it was so hot down below decks in the hold.

At 12:55 A.M. on February 3, a torpedo fired from a German U-223 submarine hit the *Dorchester*. The ship began to sink quickly. Frightened men scrambled in the darkness to reach the deck. Some were wounded and some were clothed merely in underwear against the frigid temperatures. In the confusion, lifeboats floated away without any passengers, and other lifeboats were so overcrowded that they capsized. The ship's communication system had been damaged, so none of the accompanying ships knew it was in trouble.

The chaplains stood calmly on deck. They tended to the wounded, guided the passengers to lifeboats, and convinced the men to escape the sinking vessel. Coast Guard Petty Officer John J. Mahoney recalled that his hands were freezing because he had left his gloves in his room. Lt. Goode said he had an extra pair and gave them to Mahoney. Only later did Mahoney realize that Goode had given up his own gloves so that Mahoney could stay warm.

Below the ship in the oil-slicked water, Private William Bednar floated among dead bodies. He recalled, "I could hear men crying, pleading, praying, and swearing. I could also hear the chaplains preaching courage." The chaplains' words gave him the emotional strength to swim out from under the ship and into a lifeboat.

The chaplains handed out life jackets to the men. When the supply of life jackets ran out, all four chaplains removed their own life jackets and gave them to four frightened men. Witnesses watched as the chaplains linked arms and recited prayers in English, Latin, and Hebrew, as the ship sank into the ocean's icy waters. One of the 230 survivors, John Ladd, said, "It was the finest thing I have ever seen, or hope to see, this side of heaven."

Goode, Washington, Poling, and Fox were awarded the Purple Heart and the Distinguished Service Cross after their deaths. On January 18, 1961, President Dwight Eisenhower awarded them each a Special Medal for Heroism, which has never again been awarded to anyone.

CODY'S BRAVERY

Cody Kommer of Ballston Spa, New York, was a young boy with a big sense of responsibility. He lived his short life fully. Cody was born with hydrocephalus, an excess of fluid in the brain. As he grew, he endured times of excruciating pain and multiple brain surgeries to place shunts in his brain to drain the excess fluid. Through all of his trials, he remained a child focused on others. He was extremely kind to his classmates, and they all admired him.

At school, he was placed in a special education class, but studied hard and moved to a mainstream class. He used his spring break to study with a math tutor, and even when he was hospitalized, he worked diligently on his social studies homework. He was very proud to earn a 100 percent in social studies.

Cody loved baseball and was a dedicated team member. He was not too skilled, but he practiced hard. "He was very aware of his shortcomings as a baseball player, but that never discouraged him from enjoying the game and being full of team spirit," said Cody's mother, Rose. His perseverance paid off when, after four years of playing, he got his first hit. His teammates raced from the dugout to cheer for him. Cody realized he would not become a major league player, his mother explained. Instead, he set his sights on working as a baseball announcer, so he could be closely involved with the sport.

Then, at age 15, Cody died of a brain infection. His parents donated his kidneys and liver to others because they were certain he would have wanted to give this last gift. In time, the Kommers met the man who had received one of Cody's kidneys. He was a young married man with a son and daughter. "I was so proud to know this family's life had been changed for the better," said Rose.

As reported by writer Barbara Lombardo in *The Saratogian*, Rose remembered sitting at Cody's fifth grade graduation and thinking, "There should be an award for a kid who never gives up." Now, each year at Cody's former school, Division Street School, a student who never gave up is presented with the Cody Kommer Award.

GIVING OF YOURSELF

Donating blood, bone marrow, or organs is a heroically altruistic act. The donor gives something of himself or herself for the good of others without receiving anything in return. This person is saving lives in the process. You can give blood if you are 17 years old (16 in certain states), and are at least 110 pounds (50 kilograms). Donated blood can be used to save the lives of people who have been in accidents or who are undergoing surgery. People with certain illnesses—hemophilia, for example—also require blood transfusions.

When you are 18 years old, you can decide to donate bone marrow. Bone marrow transplants can save the lives of those with leukemia, lymphoma, and other life-threatening illnesses. A small blood sample or cheek swab is all that is necessary to have your tissue type tested, and then you can add your name to the marrow donor registry. If your tissue matches someone who needs a bone marrow transplant, you will be contacted to donate. Bone marrow is removed by a surgeon after the donor is given anesthesia to numb any pain.

Some living people choose to donate organs. A kidney and a portion of the liver are examples of organs that can be given

Marissa Ayala (*standing*) was born to save her sister's life. Her parents gave birth to her in the hopes that her bone marrow would be a match for her then-19-year-old sister, Anissa (*seated*), who had been diagnosed with chronic myelogenous leukemia and needed a bone marrow transplant. Their parents' difficult decision meant that Marissa became a donor at only 14 months old. Today, the sisters—shown here in 2008—are close and proud of their story.

by a living donor. After death, many of a person's organs, such as the heart, lungs, liver, and intestines, can be removed and transplanted into the bodies of gravely ill individuals to give them an opportunity to live healthy lives. Tissues can also be donated: Corneas can be used to offer another person the gift of sight and donated skin can be used to treat burn victims.

To become an organ donor, a person should sign a donor card or check the organ donor section on his or her driver's license. Most importantly, the person must discuss his or her willingness to be an organ donor with family members because the doctors will ask them to make the final choice at the time of the donor's death.

THE HEROIC PROFESSOR

Liviu Librescu was born into a Jewish family in Romania on August 18, 1930. When Romania joined forces with Nazi Germany during World War II, Librescu and his family became victims of horrible anti-Jewish actions. He and his family were made to live in a Jewish ghetto, and Liviu's father worked in a forced labor camp.

Librescu survived the Holocaust, and after the war he studied to become an aeronautical engineer. He opposed the Communist government in Romania, so he fought to immigrate to Israel. He taught there for seven years at Tel-Aviv University. He then took a position as professor of engineering science and mechanics at Virginia Tech University in Blacksburg, Virginia.

On the morning of April 16, 2007, Virginia Tech student Seung-Hui Cho began a shooting rampage that ended with 32 people dead and 15 injured before he killed himself. At first, he killed two students in the dormitories, and then he advanced to Norris Hall, where Librescu was teaching a class on solid mechanics. When the gunman tried to enter Librescu's classroom, Librescu blocked the door with his body, which gave his students time to escape through the windows.

THE ULTIMATE GIFT

Jane Smith was a teacher in Fayetteville, North Carolina. She was constantly bugging her science student Michael Carter about pulling up his baggy pants. Finally, Michael told her that he was going through kidney dialysis, which left him sore, and that roomy pants were more comfortable for him. Michael had kidney disease and his kidneys were failing. The dialysis treatment was used to do the job of his kidneys by removing waste products from his body.

Michael told Smith he needed a kidney transplant. Smith said, "Well, I have two. Do you want one?" as reported by Emily Yellins in *The New York Times*. Miraculously, their blood types were the same, and their kidneys were a good match. Smith gave Michael her kidney and helped him return to health.

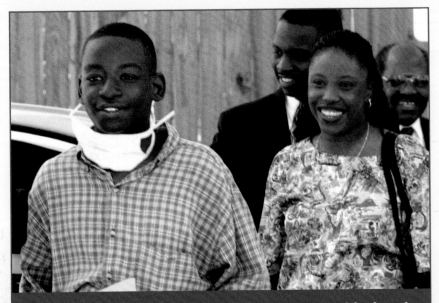

The heroic act of middle school teacher Jane Smith donating a kidney to her 15-year-old student Michael Carter (*left*) gave him a chance at a longer, healthier life. Here, Michael leaves the hospital with his mother, Deborah Evans, after a successful operation.

TEACHING UNTIL THE END

Doris Dillon was a media specialist in San Jose, California, elementary schools. She had been a teacher for 30 years when she was diagnosed with amyotrophic lateral sclerosis (ALS), commonly known as Lou Gehrig's disease. ALS is a nervous system disease that over time causes motor neurons to stop working. Motor neurons are nerve cells in the brain and spinal cord that allow a person to control his or her voluntary muscles, such as arm and leg muscles. The disease leads to the weakening and wasting away of the voluntary muscles. Ultimately, ALS affects the muscles responsible for breathing. Those suffering with ALS have a life expectancy of between three and five years.

Even with her diagnosis, Dillon bravely decided to continue to teach. She soon lost her power of speech and the ability to eat and drink. To communicate with her students, she wrote many notes and used a computer that gave voice to her words. She was determined to show by example that a disabled individual has value as a person. In addition, Dillon wanted to teach her students that death is merely a natural part of living.

According to the *Roanoke Times*, one of the students in Librescu's class, Caroline Merrey, glanced back before she jumped from the window. "I just remember looking back and seeing him at the door," she said. "I don't think I would be here without him." Librescu was shot five times as he let his students find their way to safety. For his heroism, he was awarded the Grand Cross of Romania after his death.

KEEPING GOVERNMENT RESPONSIBLE

All that is required for evil to prevail is for good men to do nothing.

—Edmund Burke (1729–1797),
British philosopher and statesman

Sometimes people decide that the United States or other countries are not acting responsibly, so they work to change the policy with which they disagree. For example, when a person commits a particularly gruesome murder, some states have the option of putting that person to death. Helen Prejean, a Roman Catholic nun with the Sisters of St. Joseph Medallle in Louisiana, is actively fighting to end the death penalty in the United States.

Prejean's public battle against the death penalty began in January 1982 when she became a pen pal to Elmo Patrick Sonnier, who was a death row inmate at the Louisiana State Penitentiary in Angola. Sonnier and his younger brother Eddie had been convicted of first-degree murder. They had kidnapped teenagers Loretta Bourque and David LeBlanc, raped Loretta, and shot them both to death. Prejean began to visit Sonnier in prison as his spiritual advisor. She got to know him as a fellow human being and did not believe he should be put to death. Prejean found him a new lawyer who fought to have his death sentence overturned. All efforts failed, and Sonnier was electrocuted on April 5, 1984.

Prejean does not think that any government has the right to put a person to death. In her book, *Dead Man Walking*, Prejean said, "No government is innocent or wise enough to lay claim to so absolute a power as death." She also pointed

Sister Helen Prejean speaks out against something about which she feels strongly: the death penalty. She is seen here in 2001 at the State Capitol Rotunda in Harrisburg, Pennsylvania, speaking at a rally to end executions in that state.

out that the United States has signed the United Nation's Universal Declaration of Human Rights, which states it is a right of every human being not to be killed or tortured. She views the death penalty as a denial of these basic rights.

As of February 2006, 123 wrongly convicted persons have been released from death row, according to Prejean's Web site. In her book, *The Death of Innocents*, Prejean said that no matter what your view is on the death penalty for those guilty of murder, no one wants an innocent individual put to death. For this reason, she thinks that the death penalty must be reconsidered. "And I say if our government is doing things we disagree with that it's only we, the people, that can hold them accountable and demand that they change because we're a democracy and democracy is hard work," said Prejean.

Prejean participates in many activities designed to share her views against the death penalty and to bring about change. She has organized "pilgrimages for life," 250-mile (400-km) walks to publicize her stance. She has written articles and books, and she gives lectures in up to 140 locations each year. Prejean believes that educating people about the death penalty will help them arrive at the same conclusion that she has.

The families of crime victims often disagree with Prejean's views on the death penalty. Elizabeth and Vernon Harvey's daughter was killed by Robert Willie, for whom Prejean served as spiritual advisor on death row. The Harveys believed that Willie deserved to die for committing such a brutal crime against their beloved daughter. They felt that he didn't deserve to live after robbing their daughter of her own life. In addition, the Harveys worried that a sentence of life imprisonment would have left the door open for Willie to murder again. Perhaps he would escape and kill, or would murder an inmate or guard in the prison. The Harveys protested in favor of the death penalty and did interviews with the media to share their opinions. Willie was executed for his crime.

YOU CAN KEEP GOVERNMENT ACCOUNTABLE

As a citizen you can make sure that the government is acting responsibly. There are ways to have your viewpoints heard. New York State Assemblyman Marc Molinaro speaks often to student groups and encourages them to become involved citizens. Most importantly, he lets students know how vital it is for them to vote once they are old enough to do so. "Every aspect of your life is impacted by people who are elected—your education, your retirement, even the local haircutter is licensed by the state," he explains. Voters should choose

A TEEN MAYOR

Marc Molinaro always had a passion for history at school. When he was a junior in high school, he attended the Presidential Classroom, a two-week program that exposed him to the workings of the federal government in Washington, D.C. In his last year of high school, he asked to intern in State Assemblywoman Eileen Hickey's office, which further sparked his interest in politics.

In Molinaro's town of Tivoli, New York, the town parks had become hangouts for drug addicts and loiterers, instead of havens for the town youth. Molinaro was discouraged by this and volunteered to serve on the town's recreation committee. While on the committee, he helped to expand T-ball and softball offerings and improved the summer recreation program.

Molinaro saw that he could make a difference in his community. So, when he was just 18 years old, he decided to run for a seat on the Tivoli Town Board of Trustees. "I thought we could use a little enthusiasm and energy," he says. He won the election, and he became the youngest person ever elected to public office in the state of New York.

issues about which they feel strongly, find a candidate whose views are in agreement with theirs, and vote for that person. Also, it is important to vote in local elections as well as in the national elections, advises Molinaro. The decisions of local officials affect your life as well.

Molinaro suggests that students should contact their public officials directly with any concerns. "We are not blessed with mind reading, so make phone calls and write letters," he says. Let your letter reflect your passion for the issue, and include some facts and statistics when you can. Don't just complain though. Also offer solutions, or volunteer your time to help fix the problem. Perhaps you can even schedule

As a trustee, he concentrated on further improving the town's recreational facilities and youth activities

The longtime mayor of Tivoli chose to retire and suggested that Molinaro run for the office. "I ran home and asked my mom if I should," says Molinaro, laughing. In 1995, he was elected mayor of Tivoli at the age of 19. He was the youngest mayor in the United States. "I was an earnest public servant, regardless of age," he says. His main focus in his 13 years as mayor was to make the town a place that made its residents proud, and to encourage residents to take an active role in town affairs. He made the center of Tivoli more people-friendly with newly paved, tree-lined streets and pedestrian walkways. He added trails and playgrounds to the parks. Tivoli became a place that towns across the state wanted to imitate.

Molinaro was elected four times to the Dutchess County Legislature. In November of 2006, he was first elected as a New York state assemblyman and was re-elected in 2008. He devotes time to speaking at schools and encouraging young people to let their voices be heard by their government. He lets them know that they, too, can make a difference.

a face-to-face meeting with your government representative. Be persistent if you don't receive a response.

If there is a problem you want to solve, find out which government official can best help you and contact that person. For example, if you want to have recycling bins placed in the town playground, you should approach the town board members or the mayor. On the other hand, if you want the federal government to increase aid to Darfur, it would be more effective to talk to your U.S. senator or congressman.

Say you want to save a 50-year-old butternut tree that your town government wants to cut down. First, you would contact the mayor or town board to express your opinion. You could also write a letter to the editor of the newspaper or a local online Web site to get support for your cause and call the local television station to see if they might want to cover the story. Circulating a petition and presenting the signed document to the local government can be an effective way to bring about change. You might organize a peaceful protest in front of the town hall. The protestors could carry informative signs, and you could invite a tree expert to speak at the demonstration. And if you really want to be certain that government is acting responsibly, consider running for public office when you are an adult, as Molinaro did.

THE FIRST LADY OF THE WORLD

Eleanor Roosevelt, the wife of U.S. President Franklin D. Roosevelt, was an activist who encouraged peace and fought for human rights for everyone all over the world. She had a specific interest in workers' rights, civil rights, and women's rights.

Roosevelt believed in the right of adults to work and to do so in the best possible work conditions. She fought against child labor and in favor of the Fair Labor Standards Act, which put an end to child labor practices. During the Great Depression, Roosevelt founded Val-Kill Furniture Factory in Hyde Park, New York. The factory made colonial-style furniture, but more importantly, it employed 60 people who desperately needed jobs.

Roosevelt took a stand for the civil rights of African Americans. In 1938, she attended the Southern Conference for Human Welfare in Birmingham, Alabama. At the conference, she was not permitted to sit with her African-American friend Mary Bethune because the audience was segregated by race. In protest, Roosevelt sat in the aisle between the African-American and white audience members. In 1939, Roosevelt resigned from the Daughters of the American Revolution because the organization refused to allow the African-American opera star Marian Anderson to perform at its Constitution Hall. Later that year, Roosevelt arranged for Anderson to sing at the Lincoln Memorial. The concert drew an audience of 75,000 people. Roosevelt also invited Anderson to perform at the White House, which was the first concert by an African American at that location.

As a young woman, Roosevelt became involved in women's causes. She was a member of the women's division of the Democratic State Committee, the Women's Trade Union League, and the League of Women Voters. When she was first lady, she held press conferences only for woman journalists. In this way, she could be sure that the media would hire woman reporters, or keep the ones they had on staff. President John F. Kennedy appointed Roosevelt the chairman of the first Presidential Commission on the Status of Women.

Eleanor Roosevelt hated war. She had witnessed the horrible results of war when she visited wounded soldiers in Europe after World War I and on the Pacific Islands during World War II. She fully supported the idea of the United Nations, which was to keep the peace between nations through diplomacy. Roosevelt served as delegate to the United Nations General Assembly from 1945 to 1952 and was appointed to that position again by President Kennedy in 1961.

One of Roosevelt's greatest achievements was serving as the chairwoman of the United Nations Human Rights

Eleanor Roosevelt brought about positive change through both her words and actions. Here, the future first lady prepares soup for unemployed women in the Grand Central Restaurant kitchen in New York City in 1932, during the Great Depression.

Commission. During this time, she helped to write the United Nations Universal Declaration of Human Rights, which was adopted December 10, 1948. This document contains 30 articles that outline basic human rights, such as freedom from slavery and freedom from torture.

Roosevelt not only brought about change through her actions, she also shared her viewpoints through words. She wrote books, articles, and magazine columns. She lectured and even had her own radio show. Much of the money she earned through this work was donated to charitable causes.

A CHILD LED THE WAY

In 1954, the U.S. Supreme Court ruled in the case of *Brown v. the Board of Education of Topeka, Kansas* that U.S. schools must be integrated. This meant that schools for white students had to allow African-American students to attend. Despite this ruling, however, white and African-American elementary school children still attended separate schools until the autumn of 1960 in New Orleans, Louisiana. The main argument was that, although the schools were separate, the education they offered was the same. This was not usually the case. For the most part, the schools for white children had more resources and could provide a better education.

Ruby Bridges was only six years old when her mother, Lucille, decided that she wanted Ruby to help integrate a white elementary school, so she could benefit from the better quality education. In Ruby Bridges's book, *Through My Eyes*, she writes that her mother said, "On the day before Ruby was born, I carried 90 pounds of cotton on my back. I wanted a better life for Ruby."

Ruby was given a challenging academic test and was chosen to be the first African-American child to integrate the William Frantz Public School in New Orleans. On November 14, 1960, U.S. federal marshals dressed in suits with armbands arrived at Ruby's home to escort her safely to school. Ruby's mother accompanied her. At the school, they were met

Ruby Bridges was only six years old when she bravely faced attending an all-white school, an act that brought about protests, hatred, and threats from those who disagreed with integration. Deputy U.S. Marshals had to escort the first grader from school in 1960.

by angry protestors yelling and throwing things. Ruby acted bravely. She said she relied on God to protect her. On that first day, Ruby and her mother sat in the school's office all day.

The next day, Ruby met her teacher, Barbara Henry, who had been newly hired specifically to teach an integrated first-grade class. However, many white parents pulled their children from the school rather than have them attend an integrated school. During that November, there were only 3 children in a school that usually taught 576, and Ruby was the only child in her class. She didn't go outside for recess and didn't have lunch with the other students.

Every morning, the protestors gathered at the school. Ruby remembered that one protestor held a black doll in a coffin, which, she said, "frightened me more than anything else." One woman even yelled that she would find a way to poison Ruby.

Through all the protests, Ruby went to school each day, and so did Barbara Henry. Ruby's teacher understood how frightening the activities outside must have been for Ruby, so she concentrated on making the classroom a safe place for learning. Ruby worked hard and earned high grades, but the principal threatened to change them. He insisted that the one-on-one attention that Ruby received resulted in grades that were higher than they should have been.

In the spring, Henry realized there was another small class of white first-graders in the school. She approached the principal and fought for and won a period during the day when the white children would study with Ruby in her classroom. Throughout the year, the other teachers and the principal would not socialize with Henry. At year's end, Henry was not invited to return to her teaching position.

Robert Coles was a psychiatrist who volunteered to work with Ruby at the time of the school's integration. "Ruby had a will and used it to make an ethical choice," Coles said. "She demonstrated moral stamina; she possessed honor and courage."

BREAKING LAWS FOR A GREATER PURPOSE

On December 7, 1941, the Japanese military bombed the U.S. Naval base at Pearl Harbor, Hawaii. The surprise attack killed 2,403 people, wounded 1,178, and sank or damaged 21 ships. The bombing was a declaration of war by Japan against the United States. As a reaction to the attack, the United States jailed 110,000 people of Japanese ancestry in prisonlike centers, known as internment camps.

Many of the Japanese people who immigrated to the United States in the early 1900s settled on the West Coast and became successful farmers. People from this generation were prohibited from becoming U.S. citizens because of the Naturalization Act of 1790. But their children, who were born in the United States, were automatically U.S.

CIVIL DISOBEDIENCE

Throughout history, civil disobedience has been used as a way to bring about change in the government. Civil disobedience is refusing to obey particular laws in a nonviolent way. Those who participate in civil disobedience must take responsibility for their actions and be prepared to accept the legal consequences.

Mohandas Karamchand Gandhi, also known as Mahatma Gandhi, was born in India on October 2, 1869. He is well known for his effective use of civil disobedience. Gandhi was a lawyer and went to work in South Africa in 1893. He was a target of anti-Indian prejudice there. For example, one day he boarded a train with a first-class ticket, but was told to move from his first-class seat. He refused and was removed from the train. Gandhi encouraged Indians in South Africa to use civil disobedience to end their oppression.

He returned to India in 1915, and again used civil disobedience to free India of British rule. For example, the British had a salt tax law that did not allow Indians to produce salt. All salt was sold by the British and was highly taxed, making it impossible for many poor Indians to purchase salt, a necessary part of their diet. Gandhi organized the salt march, a 248-mile (400-km) protest walk to Dandi, where he illegally picked up a lump of natural salt. The peaceful march had powerful implications, and it inspired many people to illegally manufacture salt throughout India. Police arrested 60,000 Indians for acts of civil disobedience in protest of the salt tax law.

citizens. People on the West coast were jealous of the Japanese because of their farming success, and this made them the target of prejudice. Following the attack on Pearl Harbor, the prejudice became even more exaggerated. People of Japanese ancestry were suspected of spying against the United States.

Gandhi also advised Indian citizens to boycott British goods, educational facilities, and courts of law. Finally, India was granted independence in 1947.

Mahatma Gandhi effectively used civil disobedience to fight for human rights, thereby positively impacting the world and inspiring future leaders such as Martin Luther King Jr. Above, Gandhi (*fourth from left*) walks with followers during the salt march in 1930.

People of Japanese descent, relocated from the Seattle area, unload their belongings as they arrive at an internment camp in Puyallup, Washington, in April, 1942. They were among thousands of people forced from their homes as the government misguidedly attempted to create national security following the attack on Pearl Harbor.

Although there was no evidence that Japanese Americans were disloyal, some high-level military officials and citizens of the states in the West wanted Japanese Americans moved. President Franklin D. Roosevelt signed Executive Order 1066 on February 19, 1942, which allowed for any person to be kept out of certain areas of the country. This opened the way for the U.S. government's internment of people of Japanese heritage.

A curfew for Japanese Americans was established. Soon after, people of Japanese ancestry—two-thirds of whom were U.S. citizens—were ordered to leave their homes for 10 "relocation centers." They were only allowed to take what they could carry. They had to sell the rest of their possessions, including houses, businesses, and cars, at rock-bottom prices.

The internment centers were surrounded by barbed wire and had towers manned by guards carrying machine guns. The barracks were so poorly made that the heat and cold, and even rodents, came in through the gaps in the floors and walls. The bathrooms lacked privacy, and people sat back to back as they relieved themselves.

A few brave Japanese Americans used civil disobedience and challenged the curfew and internment laws. Gordon Hirabayashi, a 24-year-old college student, refused to follow the internment order. He was arrested and found guilty of violating the evacuation order and curfew. He was sentenced to 90 days in prison. Minoru Yasui made his way to the police station after 8:00 P.M., purposely ignoring the curfew. He was arrested, found guilty of violating the curfew, and sentenced to a year in jail and a $5,000 fine.

Fred Korematsu also tried to fight what he thought were unfair laws. He had worked at his family's plant nursery in Oakland, California. He then held a job as a welder at a shipyard, but after Pearl Harbor was attacked, the welders union expelled him because of his Japanese heritage. He was in love with a white American woman, so he refused to be sent to

Some Japanese Americans, including Fred Korematsu (*left*), used civil disobedience to bravely fight internment and curfew laws imposed against Japanese Americans after World War II. Here, Korematsu receives a Presidential Medal of Freedom from President Bill Clinton in 1998.

an internment camp. He tried to escape detection by having eyelid and nose surgery to look less Japanese.

On May 30, 1942, Korematsu was discovered and arrested. He was tried and found guilty of violating the relocation order. The American Civil Liberties Union approached Korematsu and asked if he wanted his case to be used to test whether the internment was legal. He agreed. The U.S. Supreme Court heard the Korematsu case in 1943. Government lawyers presented "evidence" of Japanese-American spying, and the Supreme Court upheld Korematsu's conviction. The court decided that it was legal for the government to require Japanese Americans to leave certain areas of the country in order to protect national security.

However, 40 years later, in 1983, a lawyer named Peter Irons discovered documents that suggested that the government lawyers knew that the evidence of Japanese-American spying presented to the Supreme Court in 1943 was false. The Korematsu case was then tried before a U.S. district court, and Korematsu's name was finally cleared. Hirabayashi and Yasui also had their names cleared in U.S. district courts.

In 1980, the Commission on Wartime Relocation and Internment of Civilians issued a report condemning the Japanese-American internment. In 1988, President Ronald Reagan signed the Civil Liberties Act of 1988, which apologized for the U.S. government's internment of Japanese Americans and granted reparations of $20,000 to each detainee. As a follow-up in 1992, President George H.W. Bush issued a public letter to those who had been sent to the centers, and Congress set aside more funds to ensure all detainees received reparations. Finally, in 1998, President Bill Clinton presented the Presidential Medal of Freedom, the highest civilian honor, to Korematsu. "In the long history of our country's constant search for justice, some names of ordinary citizens stand for millions of souls . . .," said Clinton. "To that distinguished list, today we add the name of Fred Korematsu."

9 RESPONSIBILITY TO SELF

Love yourself, accept yourself, forgive yourself, and be good to yourself because without you the rest of us are without a source of many wonderful things.

—*Dr. Leo Buscaglia (1924–1998), author and professor*

You won't be able to take responsibility for feeding your cat or serving as coxswain for your rowing team if you don't first take care of yourself. Nothing else matters if you don't take care of your most important responsibility: your responsibility to care for yourself.

Pediatrician David Fenner considers eating well, exercising, and sleeping to be the three most important elements of being healthy. Eating good food is at the top of the list. "Food is what your body runs on and grows on," says Fenner. All parts of adolescent growth—for example, muscle and bone development—depend upon healthy eating. In addition, the strength and energy necessary for activities, such as sports, come from consuming good quality food.

In the 2006 *Pediatrics* journal article, "Dietary Recommendations for Children and Adolescents: A Guide for Practitioners," the American Heart Association and the coauthors describe which foods should be included in a healthy diet. They suggest a diet mainly of fruits and vegetables, whole grain, low fat and nonfat dairy products, beans, fish, and lean meat. The authors of the *Pediatrics* article also recommend limiting the amount of saturated and trans fat (unsaturated fat with trans isomer fatty acid), cholesterol, and added sugar and salt in the diet. The article points to the danger of consuming too many calories and becoming obese because obesity is linked to health problems, such as high blood pressure and diabetes.

Fenner offers these simple tips for choosing foods that are good for you. "The fewer words and the fewer syllables on a food's label the better," he advises. "Anytime the list of ingredients is one, such as apple or banana, it is good." In addition to eating good food, Fenner says to be careful about how much food you consume. "Moderation is key," he says. "You don't have to finish all the food."

Junk foods are made of sugars and simple starches that are stored by the body as fat, notes Fenner. He recommends choosing a piece of fruit rather than junk food snacks, such as chips and cookies. However, if you choose to have a bit of junk food, be sure to think of it as a treat and eat only a small amount. Fenner also says to drink plain water when you are thirsty, instead of sports or energy drinks, soda, or vitamin water. These types of drinks are filled with added sugar and salt, and they provide unnecessary calories to your diet.

MOVED TO MOVE

Regular exercise can help keep you physically healthy. "Exercise is what the human body was designed for," says Fenner. "The human body was designed to be moving and working all day long." Exercise helps your muscles grow and strengthen. It also helps balance the excess calories you consume because it uses them for energy.

Sitting in front of the screen and using your thumbs to play video games is not exercise, notes Fenner. On the other hand, exercise does not have to mean participation in organized

ORGANIC FOOD: THE HEALTHIER CHOICE?

O rganic foods are grown without chemical fertilizers, pesticides, growth hormones, and antibiotics. Experts are still investigating whether organically grown food is healthier for you than nonorganic products. The Mayo Clinic article, "Organic Foods: Are they Safer? More Nutritious?" argues that there are no current studies that prove organic food is more nutritious or healthier than nonorganic food.

On the other hand, in Michael Pollan's book, *In Defense of Food: An Eater's Manifesto*, he writes about the advantages of organic food. Pollan discusses research by Brian Halweil that suggests produce grown organically is richer in nutrients than produce that is grown using chemicals and industrial fertilizers. Pollan presents a theory that produce grown in organic soil requires a longer time to grow, thereby allowing it more time to absorb nutrients from the soil. Also, these plants form deeper roots, which exposes them to more of the soil's minerals.

Organic produce is not exposed to chemical pesticides, Pollan adds, so it creates the substances, called phytochemicals, it needs to protect itself from pests and disease. These phytochemicals are beneficial for human beings to consume because of their antioxidant and anti-inflammatory properties, which protect health.

The official organic label given by the U.S. government is expensive to obtain, Pollan reports. Some small local farmers may produce organic food, but may not be able to afford the official label. Therefore, food purchased from these farmers is often a healthy choice. In addition, local produce can be more nutritious than organic products grown far away, which lose some nutrients in transport.

Better yet, Pollan suggests growing your own food. That way, you can control pesticide and fertilizer use, and there won't be any nutrients lost from your backyard to your kitchen table. Another added health benefit: "Gardening can be a great stress reliever," says master gardener Ellen Kutner. "Nothing is more satisfying than to plant a seed and watch it grow."

sports. You could exercise by going for a daily walk with your friends instead of just talking to them on the telephone. You could ride a bike in the neighborhood or use an exercise machine in your home. "Build it into a routine," says Fenner.

Exercise can also contribute to your emotional well-being and keep you mentally sharp. In their study, "Exercise Is Positively Related to Adolescents' Relationships and Academics," which was published in the journal *Adolescence*, researcher Tiffany Field and her colleagues had 89 high school students complete questionnaires about their exercise habits. The participants rated their exercise level from rarely to daily. Those who reported high levels of exercise were less depressed, used drugs less frequently, and had higher grade point averages than those with low exercise levels. Field and her colleagues concluded that exercise increased the body's natural levels of serotonin, a chemical in the body that is linked to feelings of well-being. This increase in serotonin might have been the reason for the lower levels of depression among those who exercised more regularly. The researchers also made the point that an increase in serotonin level has been linked to better performance in tasks that require thinking. This might be the reason for the higher grade point averages of the students who exercised more.

SNOOZERS AREN'T LOSERS

Getting enough sleep is also a key to staying physically, psychologically, and mentally healthy. Fenner says that teenagers should sleep for nine hours or more each night. "Lack of sleep is linked to obesity, hypertension, stress, and depression," he says. "It is also believed to lower resistance to illness." In addition, Fenner says that sleep helps you grow taller, gives you energy for the day, and helps you concentrate on schoolwork.

Richard P. Millman and the American Academy of Pediatrics Committee on Adolescence explored this issue in a *Pediatrics* article entitled "Excessive Sleepiness in Adolescents and Young Adults: Causes, Consequences, and Treatment Strategies." The authors write that in a recent sample of eighth-grade students in the United States, students only received an average of 7.9 hours of sleep on weeknights, instead of the 9 to 10 hours recommended for adolescents. This lack of sleep can result in difficulties in school performance. "Studies clearly suggest that shortened sleep and irregular sleep schedules are highly associated with poor school performance for adolescents," write the authors. If you have your driver's license, that's one more reason to be sure to get your rest. The Millman article notes that driving accidents due to sleepiness are more prevalent. Those who only slept 6 to 7 hours had a 1.8 times higher risk for a sleep-related crash. If the driver had fewer that 5 hours of sleep, that risk increased to 4.5 times.

DE-STRESS, NOT DISTRESS

Everybody experiences stress now and then. Perhaps you feel stress about a major biology exam or an upcoming soccer game. However, constant feelings of stress are linked to health problems, so it is important to learn effective ways to handle stress.

So what is stress, exactly? In Joan Esherick's book, *Balancing Act: A Teen's Guide to Managing Stress,* she offers a clear explanation of what physically happens to the body during a stress reaction. Under stress, the body is preparing to react to an emergency. Imagine you are walking down the street and sense that a person is waiting in the shadows to hurt you. The body releases chemicals, called hormones, which cause the heart to beat faster so that the blood can pump to the arms and legs. The breathing rate increases, as well, bringing more oxygen into the body. The body begins to sweat to cool itself. In these ways, the body readies itself to run away or to fight. The hormones even cause the bone marrow to make more white blood cells, so the blood can clot more quickly in case the attacker wounds you. This stress reaction is perfect when someone is threatening you, but not so helpful if you're just totally panicked about a history test. If a person has this kind of stress over a long period of time, it is considered chronic stress. Chronic stress can result in physical problems, such as heart disorders and a weakened immune system.

Nancy Kelly, a clinical social worker, says that some people try to handle stress in unhealthy ways. They might turn

THE JOYS OF JOURNALING

Grabbing a pen and blank book and journaling can be good for your mental health. It can reduce stress and help you feel more optimistic. In his book, *Don't Sweat the Small Stuff for Teens*, Richard Carlson explores the benefits of recording thoughts and feelings in a journal. "The act of writing is a healthy and harmless way to sort through, ponder, reflect upon, or express your feelings," he says. Keeping a journal can bring into focus where you are in your life and where you dream to go.

If you have had a day full of frustration and sadness, Carlson says that writing the negative feelings in a journal could help you get them off your chest and relieve you of them. He suggests that if you have had a disagreement with someone and you are angry, you could write a letter to that person. Don't send it, though. Just the act of writing can make you feel calmer.

On the other hand, at the end of each day, you might write down things for which you are thankful. Carlson notes that keeping this type of gratitude journal could keep you feeling optimistic. "Focusing on all that's right with your life keeps your mind geared toward the positive aspects of life," he writes

A journal is a great place to explore your creativity, too. You can write poetry or stories, or decorate the journal pages with your paintings or photographs. In any case, make journaling fun, and you will be rewarded with health benefits.

to drinking alcohol, taking illegal drugs, or engaging in risky sexual behavior in an attempt to escape the stress. These are negative coping skills that should be avoided.

Luckily, there are many healthy ways to deal with stress. In the American Academy of Pediatrics article, "A Teen's Personalized Guide to Managing Stress," it is reported that, ". . . we can shut off the emergency system by turning on the relaxed system." Kelly suggests you might try relaxation techniques to deal with stress. One type of relaxation technique is called progressive muscle relaxation, in which you tense each of the body's muscle groups one at a time, and then relax them. Another relaxation technique is known as visualization, in which you imagine yourself in a peaceful setting, such as sitting on the beach with the waves softly lapping at your toes.

In their book, *You Staying Young*, doctors Michael Roizen and Mehmet Oz say that practicing yoga is a great stress reliever. "Yoga could very well be the ultimate de-stress technique," they write. "It lowers blood pressure and heart rate, decreases stress hormones, and increases relaxation hormones, like serotonin, dopamine, and endorphins." Interestingly, Roizen and Oz also recommended singing to relieve stress because it seems to produce relaxation hormones, as well.

Kelly advises that you could relieve stress by listening to relaxing music, taking a warm bath, or going to the movies. Calling a friend who can make you laugh or talking to a trusted adult about your stress and emotions are also good stress-reducing options. "Engage in positive self-talk," adds Kelly. "Tell yourself, 'This is something that will pass.'"

Now that you are being responsible for yourself by eating well, exercising daily, and getting plenty of sleep, you will be prepared to meet your other responsibilities. You will have the good health to handle your everyday responsibilities with some energy to spare to reach out to others.

GLOSSARY

Altruism Unselfish devotion to the welfare of others

Braille A system of raised dots that represent each letter of the alphabet, which blind individuals can read using their fingers; invented by Louis Braille in the early 1800s

Charity Generosity or helpfulness directed toward the needy or suffering

Civil disobedience Nonviolent refusal to obey laws that are seen as unfair in order to bring about change

Cyberbullying Bullying, or social cruelty, carried out online

Diligence A character trait in which the person gives an energetic effort, works hard, and does the best job possible

Flexibility The ability to change depending on the situation

Goal The target of efforts or plans

Optimism A character trait in which the person sees situations in a positive way and expects the best outcome

Perseverance The ability to continue toward a goal despite obstacles

Pessimistic A character trait in which the person sees the negative parts of situations and expects the worst outcome

Plagiarize To use another person's words without crediting the source

Priority An item that is given attention before other tasks

Procrastination To put off doing something that needs to be done

Responsible To be answerable and accountable

Self-discipline Exercising control over one's actions

Stewardship The careful and responsible management of something entrusted to one's care

Time management Organizing activities to fit into a specific time frame

BIBLIOGRAPHY

ABC News. "Parents Cyber Bullying Led to Teen's Suicide." November 19, 2007. Available online. URL: http://www.abcnews.go.com/GMA/story?id=3882520. Accessed November 9, 2008.

ALS Association. Available online. URL: http://www.alsa.org. Accessed November 9, 2008.

ALS Independence. "Teacher Views Her ALS as a Lesson." Available online. URL: http://www.alsindependence.com/Teacher_Views_Her_ALS_As_A_Lesson.htm. Accessed November 9, 2008.

American Foundation for the Blind. "Anne Sullivan Macy: Miracle Worker." Available online. URL: http://www.afb.org/AnneSullivan/default.asp. Accessed November 9, 2008.

American Foundation for the Blind. "Helen Keller." Available online. URL: http://www.afb.org/Section.asp?SectionID=1. Accessed November 9, 2008.

American Heart Association, Samuel S. Gidding, MD, chair, et al. "Dietary Recommendations for Children and Adolescents: A Guide for Practitioners." *Pediatrics* 117, no. 2 (February 2006): 544–559. Available online. URL: http://aappolicy.aappublications.org/cgi/content/full/pediatrics;117/2/544. Accessed November 9, 2008.

AmeriCorps. Available online. URL: http://www.americorps.org. Accessed November 9, 2008.

Beating Lupus. Aidan Gallagher's Story. Available online. URL: http://www.beatinglupus.org/AidenGallagher.pdf. Accessed February 4, 2009.

Bodnar, Janet. *Raising Money Smart Kids*. Chicago: Dearborn Trade Publishing, 2005.

Bolles, Richard Nelson, Carol Christen, and Jean M. Blomquist. *What Color is Your Parachute? For Teens*. Berkeley, Calif.: Ten Speed Press, 2006.

Burger, Ronald. "Pushing Forward: Disability, Basketball, and Me." *Qualitative Inquiry* 10, no. 5 (2004). Available online. URL: http://qix.sagepub.com/cgi/reprint/10/5/794. Accessed November 9, 2008.

Brady, Jonann. "Exclusive: Teen Talks About Her Role in Web Hoax That Led to Suicide." April 1, 2008. Available online. URL: http://abcnews.go.com/GMA/story?id=4560582&page=1. Accessed November 9, 2008.

Cahn, Rhoda and William Cahn. *No Time for School. No Time for Play: The Story of Child Labor in America.* New York: Julian Messner, 1972.

Caldera, Louis (former secretary of the U.S. Army, University of New Mexico law professor). Telephone interview with the author, May 2, 2008, and e-mail interview with the author, May 13, 2009.

Caldera, Louis. "Statement from Louis Caldera, Director White House Military Office, on Air Force One flight over New York." White House Press Office. Available online. URL: http://www.whitehouse.gov/the_press_office/Statement-from-Louis-Caldera-Director-White-House-Military-Office-on-Air-Force-One-flight-over-New-York/.

Carchidi, Sam. *Standing Tall: The Kevin Everett Story.* Chicago: Triumph Books, 2008.

Carlson, Richard. *Don't Sweat the Small Stuff for Teens.* New York: Hyperion, 2002.

The Carter Center. Available online. URL: http://www.carter-center.org/homepage.html. Accessed November 9, 2008.

Cauvier, Denis L., MD and Alan Lysaght. *The ABCs of Making Money 4 Teens.* Arnprior, Ontario, Canada: Wealth Solutions Press, 2005.

Cifone, Lara Kaye (Hands On! The Hudson Valley, Poughkeepsie, New York, youth services coordinator). Telephone interview with the author, June 9, 2008.

Coon, Nora E. *Teen Dream Jobs.* Hillsboro, Ore.: Beyond Words Publishing, 2003.

Cornell Law School. "U.S. Code Collection: Secretary of the Army." Available online. URL: http://www.law.cornell.edu/uscode/html/uscode10/usc_sec_10_00003013----000-.html. Accessed November 9, 2008.

Corporation for National and Community Service. "The Health Benefits of Volunteering." May 7, 2007. Available online. URL: http://www.nationalservice.gov/about/newsroom/releases_detail.asp?tbl_pr_id=687. Accessed November 9, 2008.

Covey, Sean. *The 7 Habits of Highly Effective Teens.* New York: Simon & Schuster, 1998.

de Becker, Gavin. *Protecting the Gift: Keeping Children and Teenagers Safe (and Parents Sane).* New York: The Dial Press, 1999.

Donate Life America. Available online. URL: http://www.donatelife.net. Accessed November 9, 2008.

Elliott, Lawrence. "Legends of the Four Chaplains." *Reader's Digest*, June 1989.

EurekAlert. "Study suggests too much screen time and not enough physical activity may lead to childhood obesity." April 16, 2008. Available online. URL: http://www.eurekalert.org/pub_releases/2008-04/ehs-sst041308.php. Accessed November 9, 2008.

Fenner, David. (Children's Medical Group, multiple offices in the Hudson Valley of New York, pediatrician). Telephone interview with the author, May 9, 2008.

Fetty, Margaret. *Helen Keller: Break Down the Walls!* New York: Bearport Publishing, 2007.

Field, Tiffany, Miguel Diego and Christopher E. Sanders. "Exercise Is Positively Related to Adolescents' Relationships and Academics." *Adolescence* 36, no. 141 (Spring, 2001): 105–110.

The Four Chaplains Memorial Foundation. "The Saga of the Four Chaplains." Available online. URL: http://www.fourchaplains.org/story.html. Accessed November 9, 2008.

Forbes, Kaitlin and Linda Forbes (founders of The Heart Safe Club, Rhinebeck, New York). Telephone interview with the author, December 7, 2007.

Fox News. "8 Teens Charged with Attacking Girl for YouTube Video." April 8, 2008. Available online. URL: http://www.foxnews.com/story/0,2933,347949,00.html. Accessed November 9, 2008.

Franklin D. Roosevelt Presidential Library and Museum. "Eleanor Roosevelt: 'First Lady of the World.'" Available online URL: http://www.fdrlibrary.marist.edu/erbio.html. Accessed November 9, 2008.

Freegan.info. "What is a Freegan?" Available online. URL: http://freegan.info. Accessed November 9, 2008.

Gallagher, Aiden and Elizabeth Gallagher (founders of Beating Lupus and Comforts for Chemo, Salt Point, New York). Telephone interview with the author, August 17, 2007.

Gardner, David, Tom Gardner and Selena Maranjian. *The Motley Fool Investment Guide for Teens.* New York: Fireside Book, 2002.

Ginsburg, Kenneth R. and Martha M. Jablow. "A Teen's Personalized Guide to Managing Stress." American Academy of Pediatrics. Available online. URL: http://www.aap.org/stress/buildresstress-teen.htm. Acccssed November 9, 2008.

Give Life/American Red Cross. "How to Help." Available online. URL: http://www.givelife2.org/donor/howtohelp.asp. Accessed November 9, 2008.

Gold, Susan Dudley. *Korematsu v. United States: Japanese-American Internment.* Tarrytown, N.Y.: Marshall Cavendish, 2006.

Graham, Scott. "The Salt March to Dandi." Spring 1998. Available online. URL: http://www.english.emory.edu/Bahri/Dandi.html. Accessed November 9, 2008.

Hoops, Mark (senior consumer frauds representative for the New York State Attorney General's Office). Internet safety presentation at Arlington Middle School, Poughkeepsie, New York, February 20, 2008.

Hutkins, Erinn. "Liviu Librescu: Holocaust survivor blocks shooter, lets students flee." *Roanoke Times.* April 18, 2007.

Available online. URL: http://www.roanoke.com/vtvictims/ wb/wb/xp-113497. Accessed July 7, 2009.

Isaacs, David. *Character Building: A Guide for Parents and Teachers*. Dublin, Ireland: Four Courts Press, 2001.

Jimmy Carter Library and Museum. "Biography of Jimmy Carter." Available online. URL: http://www.jimmycarter library.gov/documents/jec/jecbio.phtml. Accessed November 9, 2008.

Keller, Helen. *The Story of My Life*. New York: Doubleday & Company, 1905.

Keller, Helen. *Teacher: Anne Sullivan Macy*. Garden City, N.Y.: Doubleday & Company, 1955.

Kelly, Nancy (licensed clinical social worker with a private practice in Pleasant Valley, New York). Telephone interview with the author, May 6, 2008.

Kiyosaki, Robert and Sharon L. Lechter. *Rich Dad, Poor Dad for Teens*. New York: Warner Books, 2004.

Kommer, Rose. E-mail interview with the author, April 15, 2008.

Kutner, Ellen (owner of Simply Organized in Pleasant Valley, New York, certified professional organizer, master gardener). Interview with the author, Salt Point, New York, April 28, 2008.

Levine, Daniel, comp. "My First Job." *Reader's Digest*, March 2001.

Loomis, Carol J. "Warren Buffet Gives Away his Fortune." *Fortune*, June 25, 2006. Available online. URL: http://money. cnn.com/2006/06/25/magazines/fortune/charity1.fortune. Accessed November 9, 2008.

Louis J. Acompora Memorial Foundation. "About the Louis J. Acompora Foundation." Available online. URL: http://www. la12.org/about-foundation.html. Accessed November 9, 2008.

Lowenstein, Roger. *Buffett: The Making of an American Capitalist*. New York: Random House, 1995.

Luks, Allan and Peggy Payne. *The Healing Power of Doing Good: The Health and Spiritual Benefits of Helping Others.* New York: Fawcett Columbine, 1991.

MacLeod, Elizabeth. *Helen Keller: A Determined Life.* Tonawanda, N.Y.: Kids Can Press, 2004.

Mayo Clinic. "Organic Foods: Are They Safer? More Nutritious?" Available online. URL: http://www.mayoclinic.com/health/organic-food/NU00255. Accessed November 9, 2008.

Millman, Richard P., MD and AAP Committee on Adolescence. "Excessive Sleepiness in Adolescents and Young Adults: Causes, Consequences, and Treatment Strategies." *Pediatrics* 115, no. 6 (June 2005): 1774–1776. Available online: URL: http://aappolicy.aappublications.org/cgi/content/abstract/pediatrics;115/6/1774. Accessed November 9, 2008.

Molinaro, Marc (former mayor of Tivoli, New York, New York state assemblyman). Telephone interview with the author, April 28, 2008.

Morton, Reed W. and Stephen A. Shoop, MD "'Roswell' Star Advocates Organ Donation." Available online. URL: http://www.usatoday.com/news/health/spotlight/2002/05/15-heigl.htm. Accessed November 9, 2008.

Muellerleile, Richard (Arlington Fire District, Poughkeepsie, New York, firefighter/paramedic). Telephone interview with the author, May 5, 2008.

NASA. Official Web site. Available online. URL: http://www.nasa.gov. Accessed November 9, 2008.

National Marrow Donor Program. "Facts About Joining the Registry." Available online. URL: http://www.marrow.org/HELP/Join_the_Donor_Registry/FAQs_about_Joining_the_Registry/index.html. Accessed November 9, 2008.

New York State Department of Labor. *Laws Governing the Employment of Minors.* 2007.

Obrizok, Jennifer (Millbrook Middle School, Millbrook, N.Y., licensed school psychologist). Interview with the author, Salt Point, New York, April 27, 2008.

Okazaki, Steven. *Unfinished Business: The Japanese-American Internment Cases*. DVD. New Video Group, 2005.

Oliner, Samuel P. *Do Unto Others*. Cambridge, Mass.: Westview Press, 2003.

Oliner, Samuel P. and Pearl M. Oliner. *The Altruistic Personality: Rescuers of Jews in Nazi Europe*. New York: The Free Press, 1988.

Orman, Suze. *The Courage to be Rich*. New York: Riverhead Books, 1999.

Orman, Suze. *The 9 Steps to Financial Freedom*. New York: Crown Publishers, 1997.

Pausch, Randy and Jeffrey Zaslow. *The Last Lecture*. New York: Hyperion, 2008.

Pausch, Randy. "Carnegie Melon University: Randy Pausch's website" Available online. URL: http://download.srv.cs.cmu. edu/~pausch. Accessed November 9, 2008.

Pausch, Randy. "Time Management," lecture at the University of Virginia. November 2007. Available online. URL: http://www.youtube.com/watch?v=oTugjssqOT0. Accessed November 9, 2008.

Pollan, Michael. *In Defense of Food: An Eater's Manifesto*. New York: The Penguin Press, 2008.

Prejean, Sr. Helen. *Dead Man Walking*. New York: Vintage Book, 1993.

Prejean, Sr. Helen. *The Death of Innocents*. New York: Random House, 2005.

Roizen, Michael F., MD and Mehmet C. Oz, MD. *You Staying Young*. New York: Free Press, 2007.

Roosevelt, Eleanor. *The Autobiography of Eleanor Roosevelt*. Cambridge, Mass.: DaCapo Press, 1992.

Roosevelt, Eleanor. *On My Own*. New York: Harper & Brothers Publishers, 1958.

Roosevelt, Eleanor II. *With Love, Aunt Eleanor.* Petaluma, Calif.: Scrapbook Press, 2004.

Rosa and Raymond Parks Institute for Self Development. "Rosa Louise Parks Biography." Available online. URL: http://www.rosaparks.org/bio.html. Accessed November 9, 2008.

Ryan's Well. "Ryan's Story." Available online. URL: http://www.ryanswell.ca/story/index.html. Accessed November 9, 2008.

Scharf-Hunt, Diana and Pam Hait. *Time Management for College Students: Studying Smart.* New York: Harper Perennial, 1990.

Sharif, Iman, MD and James D. Sargent. "Association Between Television, Movie, and Video Game Exposure and School Performance." *Pediatrics* 118, no. 4 (October 2006): 1061–1070. Available online. URL: http://pediatrics.aap publications.org/cgi/reprint/118/4/e1061.pdf. Accessed November 9, 2008.

Sherman, Josepha. *Internet Safety.* New York: Watts Library, 2003.

Siegel, Danny. *Tell Me a Mitzvah.* Rockville, Md.: Kar-Ben Copies, 1993.

Spaide, Deborah. *Teaching Your Kids to Care: How to Discover and Develop the Spirit of Charity in Your Children.* New York: Citadel Press, 1995.

Stanley, Jerry. *I am an American: A True Story of Japanese Internment.* New York: Crown Publishers, 1994.

Stern, Conrad R. *The Story of Child Labor Laws.* Chicago: Children's Press, 1984.

Stimson, David. "Inner Workings of the Magnanimous Mind." National Institutes of Health. April 4, 2007. Available online. URL: http://ninds.nih.gov/news_and_events/news_articles/brain_activity_during_altruism.htm. Accessed November 9, 2008.

Wenzel, Jeffrey (Ameriprise Financial, certified financial advisor). Telephone interview with the author, May 5, 2008.

The White House. "President Bush's Cabinet." Available online. URL: http://www.whitehouse.gov/government/cabinet.html. Accessed November 9, 2008.

The White House Counsel's Office. "Memorandum for the White House Deputy Chief of Staff."

Internal Review Concerning April 27, 2009 Air Force One Flight. White House. Available online. URL:http://www.whitehouse.gov/assets/documents/Report_by_President.pdf

Willard, Nancy E. *Cyber-Safe Kids, Cyber-Savvy Teens*. San Francisco: John Wiley & Sons, 2007.

Winn, Marie. *Unplugging the Plug-In Drug: Help Your Children Kick the TV Habit*. New York: Penguin Books, 1987.

Yellins, Emily. "A Teacher's Gift? Why, Most Certainly." *New York Times,* December 18, 1999.

Youth Action International. "Kimmie Weeks." Available online. URL: http://www.youthactioninternational.org/yai/index.php/about/kimmie-weeks. Accessed November 9, 2008.

FURTHER RESOURCES

Esherick, Joan. *Balancing Act: A Teen's Guide to Managing Stress*. Philadelphia: Mason Crest Publishers, 2005.

Jones, Victoria Garrett. *Eleanor Roosevelt: A Courageous Spirit*. New York: Sterling Publishing, 2007.

Lawlor, Jennifer L. *Cyberdanger and Internet Safety: A Hot Issue*. Berkeley Heights, N.J.: Enslow Publishers, 2000.

Moss, Samantha and Lesley Schwartz. *Where's My Stuff?* San Francisco: Zest Books, 2007.

Shelley, Susan. *The Complete Idiot's Guide to Money for Teens*. IN: Alpha Books / Pearson Education Company, 2001.

Shichtman, Sandra H. *Helen Keller: Out of a Dark and Silent World*. Brookfield, Conn.: The Millbrook Press, 2002.

WEB SITES

American Foundation for the Blind: Braille Bug
http://www.afb.org/braillebug
Read about Helen Keller and the responsible life she led.

The Four Chaplains Foundation
http://www.fourchaplains.org
Read the story and biographies of the four altruistic chaplains discussed in this book.

The Giraffe Heroes Project
http://www.giraffe.org
Learn about people who "stick their necks out" for others.

My Hero Project
http://www.myhero.com
Find out about people who are living extraordinarily responsible lives.

PICTURE CREDITS

INDEX

ABOUT THE AUTHOR
AND CONSULTANTS

Marie-Therese Miller holds a bachelor's degree in psychology and a master's degree in writing from Manhattanville College. She has more than 100 published articles to her credit, including the story "Panic," found in *Chicken Soup for the Preteen Soul 2*. Miller is the author of the DOG TALES book series: *Distinguished Dogs*, *Helping Dogs*, *Hunting and Herding Dogs*, *Police Dogs*, and *Search and Rescue Dogs* (Chelsea Clubhouse, 2007). She strives to live responsibly with her husband, John, their five children, and fluffy poodle in Salt Point, New York.

Series consultant **Dr. Madonna Murphy** is a professor of education at the University of St. Francis in Joliet, Illinois, where she teaches education and character education courses to teachers. She is the author of *Character Education in America's Blue Ribbon Schools, First & Second Edition* and *History & Philosophy of Education: Voices of Educational Pioneers*. She has served as the character education consultant for a series of more than 40 character education books for elementary school children, on the Character Education Partnership's Blue Ribbon Award committee recognizing K-12 schools for their character education, and on a national committee for promoting character education in teacher education institutions.

Series consultant **Sharon L. Banas** was a middle school teacher in Amherst, New York, for more than 30 years. She led the Sweet Home Central School District in the development of its nationally acclaimed character education program. In 1992, Banas was a member of the Aspen Conference, drafting the Aspen Declaration that was approved by the U.S. Congress. In 2001, she published *Caring Messages for the School Year*. Banas has been married to her husband, Doug, for 37 years. They have a daughter, son, and new granddaughter.